Climate Change and Agriculture in Africa

This book is dedicated to the memory of Dr Helmy M. Eid, a distinguished scientist, a good friend and dedicated team member. Helmy was a passionate worrier about climate change and its impact on agriculture.

Climate Change and Agriculture in Africa

Impact Assessment and Adaptation Strategies

Ariel Dinar, Rashid Hassan, Robert Mendelsohn and James Benhin

With contributions from:

Leopold Somé, Mathieu Ouedraogo, Youssouf Dembele, Bernadette Some, Faustin Kambire, Sheick Sangare, Ernest Molua, Cornelius Lambi, Helmy Eid, Samia El-Marsafawy, Samiha Ouda, Temesgen Deressa, Abebe Tadege, Kidane Georgis, Deksyos Tarekegn, Degefie Tibebe, Jane Kabubo-Mariara, Fredrick Karanja, Katiella Maï Moussa, Moustapha Amadou, Mbaye Diop, Isidor Sene, Alioune Dieng, Wiltrud Durand, Suman Jain, Tamala Kambikambi, Reneth Mano, Charles Nhemachena (Team members)

Kenneth Strzepek, Alyssa McCluskey (University of Colorado) Matthew McCartney, Daniel Yawson (IWMI), Robina Wahaj, Florent Maraux, Giovanni Munoz Martin Smith (FAO), David Maddison (University of Birmingham), Alex Lotsch (World Bank), Pradeep Kurukulasuriya (UNDP), Nigol Seo (University of Aberdeen), Fredrik Hannerz.

With support from the World Bank

earthscan
from Routledge

First published by Earthscan in the UK and USA in 2008

For a full list of publications please contact:

Earthscan
2 Park Square, Milton Park, Abingdon, Oxfordshire OX14 4RN
711 Third Avenue, New York, NY 10017

First issued in paperback 2014

Earthscan is an imprint of the Taylor & Francis Group, an informa business

ISBN-13:   978-1-84407-547-8 (hbk)
ISBN-13:   978-0-415-85283-8   (pbk)

Typeset by Domex e-data Pvt Ltd
Cover design by Susanne Harris

A catalogue record for this book is available from the British Library

Library of Congress Cataloging-in-Publication Data
Climate change and agriculture in Africa : impact assessment and adaptation strategies / edited by Ariel Dinar ... [et al.].
     p. cm.
   Includes bibliographical references.
  1. Agriculture–Africa. 2. Climatic changes–Africa. 3. Agriculture and state–Africa. I. Dinar, Ariel, 1947–
   S472.A1C55 2008
   338.1'4096–dc22   2007041607

Contents

List of Figures, Tables and Box

Figures

Tables

Box

Acknowledgements

Major funding for the project was received from the Global Environment Facility (GEF), the Trust Fund for Environmentally and Socially Sustainable Development (TFESSD) and the Finnish Trust Fund, all within the World Bank. Complementary funding was received from the following organizations and institutions: National Oceanic and Atmospheric Administration; Office of the Global Program (NOAA-OGP); Centre for Environmental Economics and Policy in Africa (CEEPA); McArthur Foundation; Food and Agriculture Organization (FAO); International Water Management Institute (IWMI); and the University of Colorado, Boulder. We highly appreciate the Mediterranean Agronomic Institute of Zaragoza (IAMZ) for hosting the project concept meeting in 2000, and one of the project's workshops in 2004.

We benefited from constructive comments that were provided to us by Fatou Gaye, Team Leader and United Nations Framework Convention on Climate Change (UNFCCC) focal point for The Gambia; Ahmed Zakieldeen, Assistant Professor, Sudanese Institute of Environmental Studies, University of Khartoum; and Peter Cooper, Principal Scientist, International Crops Research Institute for the Semi-Arid Tropics (ICRISAT), Kenya. We also received moral support from David Kinyua, United States Agency for International Development (USAID), Kenya; Anthony Nyong, International Development Research Centre (IDRC), Kenya; Mario Herrero, International Livestock Research Institute (ILRI); and Henry Malumo, Millennium Development Goal (MDG) Campaign, Zambia. We thank all of them for their hard work related to climate change in general and to this publication in particular.

Financial support from the World Bank Institute (WBI) and from the World Bank Research Committee for dissemination of the study results are highly appreciated.

The competent administrative support provided by Dalene du Plessis and Lynette Burger of CEEPA to all project activities is highly appreciated. We thank Polly Means from DECRG for her great help in enhancing the quality of many of the figures in the book.

A project website www.ceepa.co.za/climate_change/index.html is available to provide relevant information on the project to regional and country teams and the public at large.

Foreword

This book presents a synthesis of the findings reported in a number of individual papers produced as a special series of the CEEPA Discussion Papers (www.ceepa.co.za/climate_change/index.html). They are the result of multi-country research activities conducted under the GEF-funded project: 'Climate, Water and Agriculture: Impacts on and Adaptation of Agro-ecological Systems in Africa'. The main goal of the project was to develop multipliable analytical methods and procedures to assess quantitatively how climate affects current agricultural systems in Africa, predict how these systems may be affected in the future by climate change under various global warming scenarios, and suggest what role adaptation could play. The project has been implemented in 11 countries: Burkina Faso, Cameroon, Ghana, Niger and Senegal in western Africa; Egypt in northern Africa; Ethiopia and Kenya in eastern Africa; and South Africa, Zambia and Zimbabwe in southern Africa. The study countries covered all key agroclimatic zones and farming systems in Africa. This is the first analysis of climate impacts and adaptation in the Africa continent of such scale, and the first in the world to combine cross-country, spatially referenced survey and climatic data for conducting this type of analysis.

The analyses reported in this series focus mainly on quantitative assessment of the economic impacts of climate change on agriculture and the farming communities in Africa, based on both the cross sectional (Ricardian) method and crop response simulation modelling. The cross sectional analysis also allowed for assessing the possible role of adaptation. Moreover, the project employed river-basin hydrology modelling to generate additional climate attributes for the impact assessment and climate scenario analyses such as surface runoff and stream flow for all districts in the study countries.

CEEPA coordinated all project activities in close collaboration with many agencies in the involved countries, the Agriculture and Rural Development (ARD) Department and the Development Economics Research Group (DECRG) of the World Bank, the WBI, FAO, Yale University, the University of Colorado and IWMI.

All opinions presented in this book and any errors in it are those of the authors and do not represent the opinion of any of the above listed agencies.

List of Acronyms and Abbreviations

ACRU	Agrohydrological Model of the Agricultural Catchments Research Unit (South Africa)
AOGCM	atmospheric-oceanic global circulation model
ARD	Agriculture and Rural Development (*World Bank Department*)
ARTES	Africa Rainfall and Temperature Evaluation System
BLS	Basic Linked Systems
CCC	Canadian Climate Centre
CCCM	Climate and Carbon Cycle Modelling
CCSR	Centre for Climate System Research
CEEPA	Centre for Environmental Economics and Policy in Africa
CERES	Crop Estimation through Resource and Environment Synthesis
CROPWAT	Crop Water
CROPWATCC	Crop Water with Climate Change
DEM	digital elevation model
ENSO	El Niño-Southern Oscillation
FAO	Food and Agriculture Organization
FRIEND	Flow Regimes from International Experiments and Network Data
GCM	general circulation model
GDP	gross domestic product
GEF	Global Environment Facility
GENESIS	Global Environment and Ecological Simulation of Interactive Systems
GFDL	Global Fluid Dynamics Laboratory
GISS	Goddard Institute for Space Studies
GNP	gross national product
GRDC	Global Runoff Data Center
IAMZ	Mediterranean Agronomic Institute of Zaragoza

IBSNAT	The International Benchmarks Sites Network for Agrotechnology Transfer
ICRISAT	International Crops Research Institute for the Semi-Arid Tropics
IDRC	International Development Research Centre
IFC	International Finance Corporation
ILRI	International Livestock Research Institute
IPCC	Intergovernmental Panel on Climate Change
IWMI	International Water Management Institute
MDG	Millennium Development Goal
MoA	Ministry of Agriculture
MoFA	Ministry of Food and Agriculture
NDA	National Department of Agriculture
NOAA-OGP	National Oceanic and Atmospheric Administration; Office of the Global Program
PCM	Parallel Climate Model
POLD	Pollard and Thompson – GENESIS with dynamic sea-ice
STATA	Statistics/data Analysis
TFESSD	Trust Fund for Environmentally and Socially Sustainable Development
TTL	task team leader
UCL	University College, London
UIUC	University of Illinois at Urbana-Champaign
UKMO	United Kingdom Meteorological Office
UNFCCC	United Nations Framework Convention on Climate Change
UNH	University of New Hampshire
USAID	United States Agency for International Development
USDA	United States Department of Agriculture
USGS	United States Geological Survey
WATBAL	Water Balance
WBI	World Bank Institute
WRSI	water requirements satisfaction index

Introduction and Rationale

Current evidence (IPCC, 2001, 2007) suggests that countries in temperate and polar locations may enjoy small economic advantages because additional warming will benefit their agricultural sectors. Many countries in tropical and subtropical regions are expected to be more vulnerable to warming because additional warming will affect, among other things, their dwindling water balance and harm their agricultural sectors. The problem is expected to be most harsh in Africa where current climate is already severe, current information is the poorest, technological change has been the slowest and the domestic economies depend most heavily on agriculture. African farmers have adapted to some extent to climate variability, but climate change may well force large regions of marginal agriculture in Africa out of production (Kurukulasuriya et al, 2006).

Even without climate change, there are serious concerns about agriculture in Africa because of water supply and water variability. Figure 1.1 (see also plate 1) provides both the spatial means and the inter-temporal variation of rainfall in the continent. Vast sections of Africa do not have enough water to support crops, and these same areas are highly vulnerable to water variability. Drought events are common in Africa (Figure 1.2). The number of people affected by drought in Africa is nearly equal to the entire world population affected by drought in certain years. Climate change is expected to aggravate these impacts.

A number of countries in Africa already face semi-arid conditions that make agriculture challenging. Further, development efforts have been particularly difficult to sustain. African agriculture has the slowest record of productivity increase in the world. Experts are concerned that the agriculture sector in Africa will be especially sensitive to future climate change and any increase in climate variability. The current climate is already marginal with respect to precipitation in many parts of Africa. Further warming in these semi-arid locations is likely to be devastating to agriculture there. Even in the moist tropics, increased heat is expected to reduce crop yields. Agronomic studies (in this volume) suggest that yields could fall quite dramatically in the absence of costly adaptation measures. The current farming technology is basic, and incomes low, suggesting that farmers will have few options to adapt. Presently, public infrastructure such as roads, irrigation systems, long-term weather forecasts, and agricultural research and extension are inadequate to secure appropriate adaptation. Unfortunately, none of the empirical studies of climate impacts in Africa has explored what adaptations would be efficient for either African farmers or African governments.

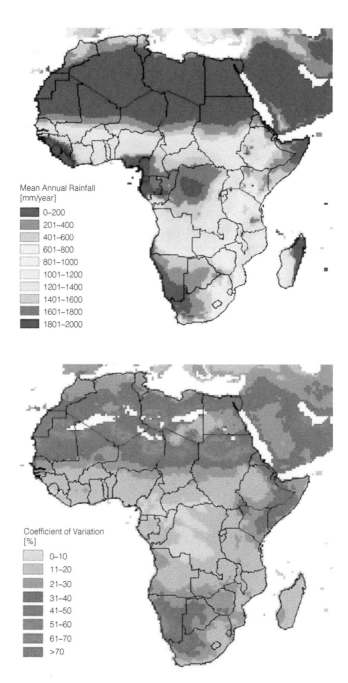

Figure 1.1 Africa: Mean annual total precipitation (mm/year) (top) and coefficient of variation (%) (bottom) derived from University of East Anglia Climate Research Unit (UEA-CRU) 1951–2000 monthly time series

Note: See plate 1 for a colour version of this figure.
Source: Lotsch (2006)

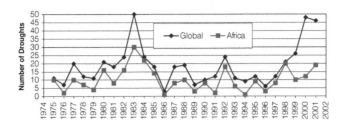

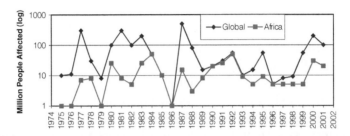

Figure 1.2 Number of drought events (top) and population affected by drought (bottom) globally (diamonds) and in Africa (squares) during 1975–2001 (*x*-axis). People affected are defined as requiring immediate assistance

Source: Based on Office of US Foreign Disaster Assistance/Centre for Research on the Epidemiology of Disasters (OFDA/CRED) International Disaster Database (www.cred.be/emdat)

This is a serious deficiency in African impact research, given the likely importance of efficient adaptation to the continent (Mendelsohn, 2000).

Although there are well-established concerns about climate change effects on agriculture in Africa, there is little quantitative information on how serious these effects will be. Existing studies by the year 2000 covered only a small fraction of Africa and focused on a handful of countries. In addition, few of the African studies included data on and analysis of actual farmer behaviour (i.e. adaptation, which includes responses such as planting dates, harvest dates, use of fertilizer and crop choice). Existing studies have mostly examined how individual crops behave in controlled experiments, addressing largely grain crops (see literature review in Annex 1 and Kurukulasuriya and Rosenthal, 2003). By using results of controlled experiments, researchers could estimate coefficients that measure climate change impact on crop yield that, in association with market prices, could provide experimental-based impact estimates. For a more detailed discussion about crop experiments and their use in estimating impact of climate change on crops, as well as other approaches to estimating impact of climate change on agriculture, see Chapter 3.

A first attempt to evaluate the likely impact of climate change on the agricultural sector in Africa on a continent-wide scale (Mendelsohn et al, 2000)

had to rely on studies about climate sensitivity that have been performed in the United States (Mendelsohn et al, 1994, 1996; Mendelsohn and Neumann, 1999). Because local African studies have not yet calibrated climate sensitivity, these initial estimates were highly tentative, but provided a sense of the uncertainty surrounding African forecasts.

We present results that used response functions calibrated from experimental models in the US. Forecasts of agricultural impacts in billions of dollars for the year 2100 for each country using 14 different climate models are presented in terms of percentage of gross domestic product (GDP) (base agricultural GDP year is 1990; Figures 1.3a, b, plates 2 and 3). The experimental response function is more climate sensitive and leads to larger benefits in the polar region and larger damages in the low latitudes compared with the cross sectional results. The figures contain a picture of the average effect across all 14 general circulation models (GCMs), as well as the most optimistic and the most pessimistic results. The most optimistic climate model, Pollard and Thompson – Global Environment and Ecological Simulation of Interactive Systems (GENESIS) with dynamic sea-ice (POLD), predicts a modest increase in temperature near the equator and a larger increase in the temperate zones and near the poles (Thompson and Pollard, 1995). The most pessimistic climate model, University of Illinois at Urbana-Champaign (UIUC), predicts significant warming near the equator and moderate warming near the poles (Schlesinger and Zhao, 1989). These different temperature and precipitation forecasts have important implications for the climate in Africa. However, all the models show that Africa is the most vulnerable continent in the world to climate change.

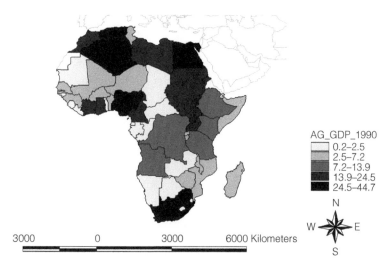

Figure 1.3a Agricultural GDP of African countries in 1990 (AG_GDP_1990) in billions of 1990 US$

Note: See plate 2 for a colour version.
Source: Mendelsohn et al (2000)

The results in Figure 1.3b suggest the likely continent-wide impact of 6–100 per cent reduction in GDP in 2100, except for two or three countries projected to benefit from climate change. These predictions depend on experimental results from the agronomic literature. We also examined predictions that come from the results of cross sectional comparisons across US farms. The results show

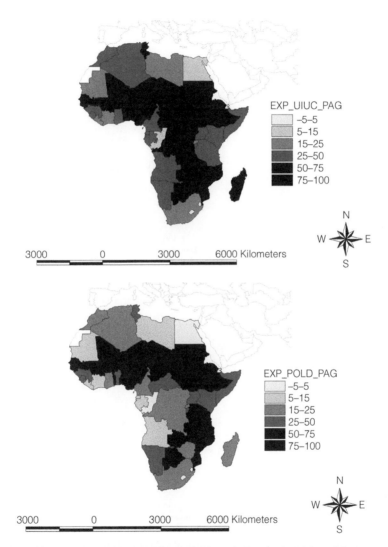

Figure 1.3b Percentage change in agricultural GDP in 2100 in African countries due to climate change, using the UIUC and POLD global climate change models and experimental (EXP) coefficients. Values on the top and bottom panels are based on the UIUC and POLD model runs, respectively (positive values mean loss and negative values mean gain)

Note: See plate 2 for a colour version.
Source: Mendelsohn et al (2000)

a similar response by African agriculture to future climate scenarios, but the effects are much smaller (Figure 1.3c, plate 4). The results in Figure 1.3c suggest that the impacts are much less severe, ranging between 6 and 60 per cent of GDP in 2100, and that more countries would benefit from climate change.

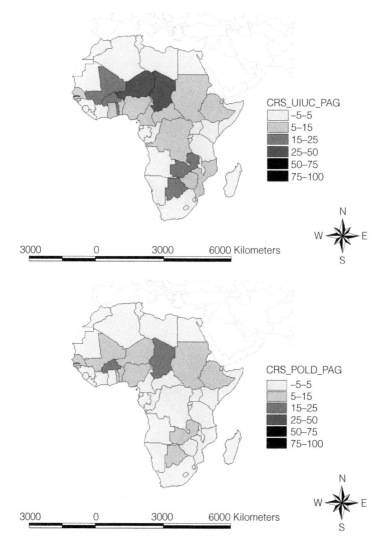

Figure 1.3c Percentage change in agricultural GDP in 2100 in African countries due to climate change, using the UIUC and POLD global climate change models and cross sectional (CRS) coefficients. Values on the top and bottom panels are based on the UIUC and POLD model runs, respectively (positive values mean loss and negative values mean gain)

Note: See plate for a colour version.
Source: Mendelsohn et al (2000)

The results in Figure 1.3c suggest that with cross sectional coefficients (that take into account adaptation), impacts are much less severe, although they range between 6 and 60 per cent of GDP in 2100. However, more countries in this analysis will benefit from climate change.

The overall results (Figures 1.3b and 1.3c) indicate that the climate sensitivity of agriculture in Africa is important. Even relying upon a single climate model, UIUC, the impacts in Africa as a continent can range from a potential loss of $25 billion[1] to a loss of $194 billion per year, depending on the climate sensitivity used. The most pessimistic forecast comes from the experimental simulation data that suggest that African countries may lose 47 per cent of their agricultural revenue because of global warming. However, this forecast is possibly extreme because only limited adaptation is included in the model, and the theoretical models in this case do not contain any tropical crops. The cross sectional forecast was less pessimistic, suggesting losses of only 6 per cent of agricultural GDP. These numbers are more moderate because cross sectional models automatically include a comprehensive set of adaptation measures. It is likely that the correct estimates for Africa are bounded by these two US-based estimates. However, even this is uncertain because the US results are calibrated to a temperate climate and US farmers use more capital-intensive agricultural technologies than farmers in Africa.

Nevertheless, these results are sufficiently indicative of how African agriculture may be very vulnerable to climate change. The modelling results presented here indicate that the potential damages may be large both in absolute terms and as a fraction of agricultural GDP. However, even these impact estimates may be optimistic because they were based on US climate response functions. While the predictions presented here may look irrelevant nowadays due to availability of new procedures and data, they were alarming, especially when combined with other problems facing African countries, such as slow technological change, poor information availability, high dependency of the economy on agriculture and lack of appropriate institutions. These problems are severe even without climate change.

A first response to these results was the recognition that Africa needs an immediate and comprehensive analysis of likely climate change impacts and adaptation options.[2] The need for analysis was transformed into a series of multi-country research activities conducted under the Global Environment Facility- (GEF-) funded project: 'Climate, Water and Agriculture: Impacts on and Adaptation of Agro-ecological Systems in Africa'. The main goal of the project was to develop multipliable analytical methods and procedures to assess quantitatively how climate affects current agricultural systems in Africa, predict how these systems may be affected in the future by climate change under various global warming scenarios, and what role could adaptation play. The project has been implemented in 11 countries: Burkina Faso, Cameroon, Ghana, Niger and Senegal in western Africa; Egypt in northern Africa; Ethiopia and Kenya in eastern Africa; and South Africa, Zambia and Zimbabwe in southern Africa. The study countries covered all key agroclimatic zones and farming systems in Africa. This is the first analysis of climate impacts and adaptation in the Africa continent of such scale, and the first in the world to combine cross-country, spatially referenced survey and climatic data for conducting this type of analysis.

This book focuses mainly on the policy implications of the quantitative assessment of the economic impacts of climate change on agriculture and the farming communities in Africa, based on both the cross sectional (Ricardian) method and crop response simulation modelling. The cross sectional analysis allowed also for assessing the possible role of adaptation. In addition, the study employed river-basin hydrology modelling to generate additional climate attributes for the impact assessment and climate scenario analyses such as surface runoff and stream flow for all districts in the study countries.

An important observation that should be added to our work is that Africa is already undergoing fundamental changes, not related to climate change, that are driven by (a) population growth, (b) continuing natural resource degradation (especially decline in soil fertility), (c) change and/or loss of natural ground cover and (d) rural to urban migration. The research presented in this book has taken the already existing processes as given and does not address the interaction between such ongoing changes and future climate change. Some aspects of these ongoing changes are addressed in our conclusions and policy implications in Chapter 6.

The remainder of the book is organized as follows. Chapter 2 spells out the objectives of the study, and the structure and organization of the team, including the role of and interaction among the various international organizations that participated. In particular, sampling the different countries is explained to show how the study captures the distribution of the agro-ecological zones of the continent. The chapter mentions briefly the four methods used in the analysis: the Ricardian approach and crop response simulation modelling, which were intended to generate estimates of the quantitative impacts of climate change; a hydrological modelling that supplements the analysis by providing runoff and flow estimates; and a method employing micro-economic modelling to identify how African farmers have already adapted to climate change. The chapter also provides information on the data collection and documentation of the results. Chapter 3 explains the various methods used and how they are integrated into one analysis. Chapter 4 offers country-level results of the various methods applied. Each country's results are scrutinized separately through all four applied methods. Chapter 5 focuses on regional results combining the data from all participating countries. Looking at the agronomic impacts, economic impacts, hydrological analysis and perception results from a regional point of view, there are several policy issues that are highlighted. In addition, the regional analysis allows consideration of more aspects than in the country-level analysis.

Therefore, issues such as substitution among inputs, investment and so on are well within the capacity of the analysis to address. Chapter 6 concludes and spells out the main policy messages of this project for Africa and for the international community. This is especially relevant if the policy community needs to begin adaptation projects in Africa. Although this study began to identify how farmers adapt to warmer and drier/wetter locations, adaptation remains an area that clearly needs more research and capacity. The study began to identify which areas in Africa are more vulnerable to future climate changes, but more research must be done to refine these forecasts.

Notes

1. Dollars are US currency throughout the book.
2. We would like to highlight a concern raised by one of our reviewers about the possible confusion between 'coping' with seasonal weather changes and 'adaptation' to long-term climate change. *Coping Strategies* are defined as strategies that have evolved over time through people's long experience in dealing with the known and understood natural variation that they expect in seasons combined with their specific responses to the season as it unfolds. *Adaptive Strategies* are defined as longer-term (beyond a single season) strategies that are needed for people to respond to a new set of evolving conditions (biophysical, social and economic) that they have not previously experienced.

2

Study Objectives, Structure, Methodology, Organization and Countries' Agroclimatic Conditions

The study was aimed to develop replicable analytical methods and procedures for assessing the impact of climate change on agriculture in Africa, to estimate how climate affects the current agricultural systems and to project how climate change may affect these systems in the future. The study had the following specific objectives:

• national-level economic analyses of impacts and adaptation;
• cross-national (regional) analyses, including impact of water supply, with results extrapolated to cover countries not included in the sample;
• enhancement of the capacity of country experts;
• facilitation of an intra-country exchange of findings and policy alternatives, among various levels of decision makers from each country;
• development of inter-country exchanges between all the country teams participating in the study.

The following outcomes were expected from the study:

• a quantitative estimation of the national and regional impacts of climate change in the agricultural sector;
• identification of national and regional adaptation measures used in response to impacts of climate change on the agricultural sector;
• development of databases and models to predict how climate change will impact the agriculture sector and how the agricultural sector will adapt;
• improved expertise in the sample countries.

In order to achieve these objectives, the study developed a methodology including sampling of countries in the continent in such a way that the results could be applied to any country in the continent.

Structure and organization of the study

The project involved task team leaders (TTLs) from the World Bank, a project implementation agency, and regional and country research teams. The TTLs were responsible for the general overseeing of the project with respect to project research proposals and the structure of reports and the assessment and approval of regional and country research team members. The implementing agency team, Centre for Environmental Economics and Policy in Africa (CEEPA), included a project leader, project coordinator, project administrator and project workshop coordinator. The team was responsible for the day to day running of the project and ensuring that specific objectives and outcomes defined in the project document were achieved. The project implementation agency was also the main liaison between the country and regional research teams in each country, and the TTLs.

The regional teams consisted of the following research groups: Economic Impact Assessment from Yale University, Crop Response Simulation Modelling from the Food and Agriculture Organization (FAO), River-Basin Hydrology Modelling from the International Water Management Institute (IWMI) and the University of Colorado, Boulder, and the Perception and Adaptation to Climate Change from University College, London (UCL). Country teams from each of the 11 countries were made up of economists, agronomists, hydrologists and postgraduate students. It was envisaged that the postgraduate students would use some of the datasets collected for the project for their dissertations, and by doing so would also build capacity in this area.

The leaders of each of the regional and country research teams were pre-selected based on their capacity and leadership. The other members of the teams were selected by the team leaders in collaboration with CEEPA, and subsequent assessment and approval by the Bank. Each country team was responsible for: (a) conducting the country analysis, which involved designing, sampling and data collecting, and carrying out the country level analysis of the climate change impacts on the agricultural sector, and of local adaptation; (b) presenting results of the country analysis at the project workshops; and (c) producing the various country reports for the project. The team leader had the responsibility of ensuring that these activities were undertaken.

As part of the implementation of the country studies, each country prepared a country-level research proposal based on the project document, with the direction of CEEPA, which was assessed and approved by the Bank. Country proposals consisted of the following: (a) contribution of the country study to the overall objectives (capacity building and research) of the project; (b) tasks and deliverables for achieving the set goals; (c) adaptation of the proposed methodology for the country study; (d) data sources and expected data collection problems; (e) inclusion of different disciplines (economics, agronomy,

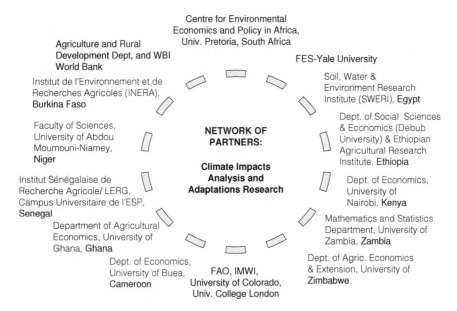

Figure 2.1 Make-up of the project and its sponsors

Source: Kurukurasuriya, 2004

hydrology) and, as possible, inclusion of graduate students; (f) work plan and time line for completion of specific tasks; and (g) research teams (with their CVs) and budget allocations (time and money). Each of the regional teams followed the same process. The make-up of the project and its sponsors is presented in Figure 2.1.

Capacity building and training workshops

The overall objective of the training workshops was to ensure consistency in the approach and necessary quality control of country-level and regional assessments of the vulnerability of African agriculture to climate change, and adaptation options, as well as to build and strengthen sustainable local capacity to address these aspects.

Three annual training workshops and two technical training workshops were held over the project period: (a) A 'Launching and training workshop on unified methodologies and data collection needs' was held in Cape Town, South Africa, 4–7 December 2002. The workshop reviewed, and introduced country research teams to, the three principal methodological approaches: Cross sectional, crop simulation modelling and hydrological modelling; (b) A 'Technical training workshop on crop response simulation and river basin hydrology modelling' was held in Accra, Ghana, 23–26 June 2003. It trained country teams on the application of the Crop Water (CROPWAT) and Water Balance (WATBAL) models and finalized plans for implementing country level analyses; (c) A 'Training workshop on quality control for country level and regional analysis and reporting' was held in Cairo, Egypt, 10–13 November 2003. This workshop followed the completion of in-country field surveys and data collection, and sought to promote consistent quality of country analyses and reporting, and correct possible methodological problems. Participants were also trained in the use of Statistics/data Analysis (STATA), a statistical and econometric package, which was utilized for the cross sectional analyses; (d) A 'Technical training workshop on the implementation of the cross sectional analysis' was held in KwaZulu Natal, South Africa, 3–6 May 2004, and concentrated on further training on the country-level Ricardian statistical analyses using STATA; (e) An 'Understanding and adapting to climate change: What can the world learn from Africa's experience' workshop was held at the Mediterranean Agronomic Institute of Zaragoza (IAMZ), Zaragoza, Spain, 13–16 December 2004 and focused on (i) a rigorous review and critical evaluation of the preliminary empirical results of the national studies, providing suggestions for improving the analyses and interpretation of study results and findings and their policy implications, and (ii) review and evaluation of results of the regional assessment studies on the potential economic and hydrological impacts and crop responses of climate change on agro-ecosystems in Africa, and the various adaptation options.

Methodology and country selection

The study promoted data collection and analysis of baseline climate change impact and adaptation based on cross section models (Chapter 3). Cross section models use data from various locations to infer and assess behaviour of farmers and impacts across different climates. These models allow quantitative estimates of the economic impact of climate change in the sampled locations in each country. To provide benchmark values of major crop yields and their response to climate change, the FAO crop model (CROPWAT) simulated yields under existing climates (Chapter 3). A hydrological model, developed by the University of Colorado in collaboration with IWMI (Chapter 3), produced necessary runoff and stream flow values in the sampled locations.

In order to estimate the cross section models, it was necessary to collect baseline climatic data, agricultural production data and water flow data for each sampled district in each country. The data allow the approach to estimate the economic outcome of farms facing different climate and water supplies. By comparing farm net incomes across climates, one can estimate the climate sensitivity of current farms in each country. The information provided was then used to predict the long-run impacts of both small changes in climate and future climate scenarios. By comparing the choices farmers make in different climates, one can also begin to understand effective adaptation measures. By using general circulation model (GCM) results, it is possible to predict the impacts of different future climate scenarios for each country and to evaluate how agriculture is likely to adapt.

There are eight agro-ecological zones in Africa. The selected countries cover all these agro-ecological zones and the farming systems in the continent (FAO, 2001). Districts were selected within each country to further increase the representation across climate zones. The sample selection process provides good coverage across climate zones and vegetation types (Chapter 4) of all the countries in the continent (see Table 2.1, Table 2.2 and Figure 2.2, plate 5). It is therefore possible to extrapolate the outcome of the study to cover the whole continent.

This sample selection process also led to a good distribution of countries across the geography and political spectrum of Africa. Countries from each region of the continent are included. Countries with different racial, religious and language backgrounds are also represented. A short description of the

Table 2.1 *Distribution of farming systems in the agro-ecological zones in Africa*

Agro-ecological zone	Farming system	% of land area	Agricultural pop (%) of total in the region
Various	Irrigated	1	2
Humid	Tree crop	3	76
	Forest based	11	7
	Rice-tree crop	1	2
	Highland perennial	1	8
Humid/temperate	Highland temperate mixed	2	7
Moist sub-humid	Root crop	12	12
Dry sub-humid	Cereal root crop mixed	13	15
	Maize mixed	10	16
	Large commercial and small holder	5	5
Semi-arid	Agro-pastoral Millet	8	9
Arid	Pastoral	14	7
	Sparse (arid)	18	2
Various	Coastal artisanal fishing	2	3
	Urban based	Little	Little

Table 2.2 *Africa: Farming system characteristics of selected countries*

Country	Agro-ecological system
Burkina Faso	8, 11
Cameroon	2, 3, 7
Egypt	8, 11, 12
Ethiopia	5, 6, 9, 12
Ghana	2, 7, 8
Kenya	9, 11, 12
Níger	12, 13
Senegal	1, 11
South Africa	9, 10, 13
Zambia	1, 7, 8, 9, 11
Zimbabwe	9, 11, 12, 13

Legend: (1) Irrigated (2) Tree crops (3) Forest based (5) Highland perennial (6) Highland temperate mixed (7) Root crop (8) Cereal root crop mixed (9) Maize mixed (10) Large commercial and small holder (11) Agro-pastoral millet/sorghum (12) Pastoral (13) Arid.

Source: FAO (2001)

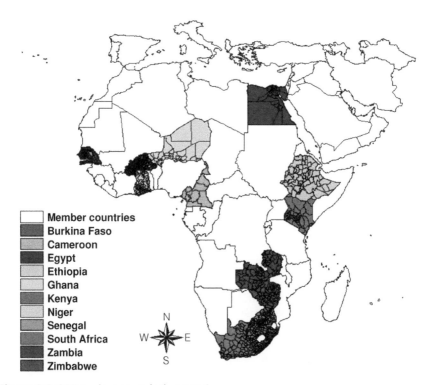

Figure 2.2 GEF project sampled countries

Note: See plate 5 for a colour version.
Source: Strzepek and McCluskey (2006)

regions and their distribution over the continent are provided in Table 2.1, Table 2.2 and Figure 2.2.

Although we do not have a precise measure of the share of these agro-ecological zones in our sample countries, Figure 2.3 (plate 6) suggests that they are accurately represented in the sample. Given the representative spread of the sample, it was possible to extrapolate the outcome of the study to cover the whole continent.

Geography and climate setting

The climate in Africa is predominantly tropical, and broadly classified into three main climatic zones: humid equatorial, dry, and humid temperate. Within these broad zones, altitude and other localized variables also produce eight distinctive regional climates: tropical rainforests, humid subtropical, Mediterranean, tropical savanna, steppe, desert, highland and marine (Figure 2.3) (Lamousé-Smith and School, 1998). The climates are described below.

Tropical rainforest climate is characterized by heavy rainfall, very high humidity and high temperature all year round. There is little variation in seasons. The coldest month has a temperature range above 18°C and the driest month has at least 6000mm of precipitation.

Humid subtropical climate occurs on the south-eastern coast of the continent. It receives rainfall year round with the heaviest amount during the summer. The warmest month has a temperature range above 10°C and the coldest month ranges between 0°C and 18°C.

Mediterranean climate is characterized by dry hot summers and wet mild winters. The warmest month has temperatures above 10°C; the coldest month ranges between 0°C and 18°C. The driest month occurs in the summer between December and March.

Tropical savanna climate (sometimes referred to as tropical wet-and-dry) is characterized by a rainfall season of up to six months (May–October) (wet summer) followed by dryness (in winter). There is also uneven rain distribution with more towards rainforest and less towards desert. The coldest month has a temperature range above 18°C.

Steppe climate includes the desert areas with climatic conditions similar to those found in the desert climate. It is semi-arid and hot with very high temperatures. Very slight rainfall may occur in a few areas. Annual precipitation is relatively low with precipitation less than half of potential evapotranspiration.

Desert climate is characterized by extreme heat and aridity caused by stagnant continental air masses. Annual precipitation is relatively low with precipitation less than half of potential evapotranspiration.

Highland climate is similar to the savanna climate in the low lying areas adjacent to the highlands. The high altitudes of the mountains moderate the temperatures to make them warm and temperate. Due to increased elevation,

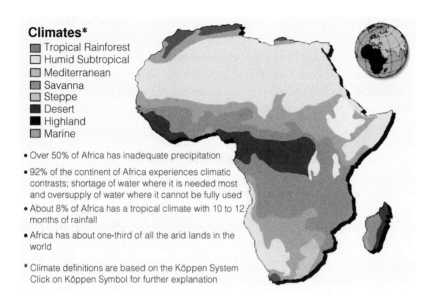

Climates*

- ■ Tropical Rainforest
- □ Humid Subtropical
- □ Mediterranean
- ■ Savanna
- □ Steppe
- ■ Desert
- ■ Highland
- ■ Marine

- Over 50% of Africa has inadequate precipitation
- 92% of the continent of Africa experiences climatic contrasts; shortage of water where it is needed most and oversupply of water where it cannot be fully used
- About 8% of Africa has a tropical climate with 10 to 12 months of rainfall
- Africa has about one-third of all the arid lands in the world

* Climate definitions are based on the Köppen System
Click on Köppen Symbol for further explanation

Figure 2.3 Africa: Main climatic zones

Note: See plate 6 for a colour version.
Source: www.courses.psu.edu/aaa_s/aaa_s110_tah/AFIM/Main_HTML/M_CL.html

climates in the highlands are cooler than those around them. Also due to the increased elevation, climates in the highlands are wetter than those around them.

Marine climate, like the humid subtropical climate, occurs on the south-eastern section of the continent. It receives rainfall year round with the heaviest amount during the summer. Warmest temperature is in a range above 10°C and the coldest month ranges between 0°C and 18°C.

Associated with the different climatic zones are nine different vegetation zones: desert; semi-desert and desert steppe; tropical woodland and grassland savanna; tropical broadleaf woodland savanna; oasis vegetation; tropical rainforests; mountain vegetation and temperate grassland; Mediterranean forest and scrub; and the Sahel (Figure 2.4, plate 7) (Lamousé-Smith and School, 1998). They are described below.

Desert vegetation is mostly barren, has rocky or sandy surface, no vegetation except for a few plants that have adapted to the limited water supply.

Semi-desert and desert steppe vegetation is seen in highly fertile brown or black soil covered by short grasses or shallow rooted plants and shrubs.

Tropical woodland and grassland savanna vegetation consists of low growing groups of deciduous and evergreen trees and shrubs, with many species bearing thorns. Due to severe dry seasons, grasses are almost absent.

Tropical broadleaf woodland savanna vegetation is characterized by having tall trees (15–20m), and tall perennial grasses that border tropical forests.

Oasis vegetation is associated with irrigated zones from a locally exotic stream or underground water supply.

Tropical rainforest has the richest biomes in terms of number of species of plants. The forests are dominated by broadleaf evergreen trees, which have thick leaves but relatively thin bark. Forests are made up of three to four layers of trees according to height, with the top layer reaching 45–55m. Tropical forests also contain many species of ferns, vines and shrubs.

Mountain vegetation and temperate grassland is relatively low forest, made up of twisted trees that seldom exceed 9–12m. An abundance of mosses and lichens covers most plants. The higher elevations are dominated by grasses and shrubs.

Mediterranean forest and scrub is evergreen mixed forest of coniferous and broadleaf trees with small shrubs scattered throughout. Oaks and pines are common to these forests.

The Sahel is a broader region along the southern margin of the Sahara Desert. It is a region that is in transition from tropical grassland to desert, a phenomenon also known as desertification. The area is semi-arid with occasional clumps of short grasses and thorns that are sparsely scattered on the largely barren landscape.

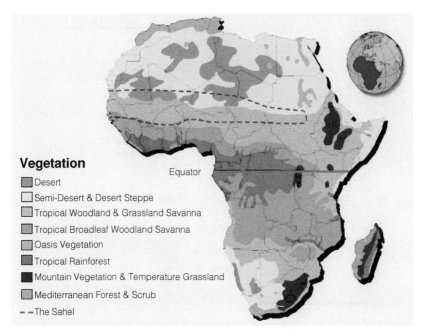

Vegetation
Equator
- ◼ Desert
- ◻ Semi-Desert & Desert Steppe
- ◼ Tropical Woodland & Grassland Savanna
- ◼ Tropical Broadleaf Woodland Savanna
- ◼ Oasis Vegetation
- ◼ Tropical Rainforest
- ◼ Mountain Vegetation & Temperature Grassland
- ◼ Mediterranean Forest & Scrub
- – – The Sahel

Figure 2.4 Africa: Types of vegetation

Note: See plate 7 for a colour version.
Source: www.courses.psu.edu/aaa_s/aaa_s110_tah/AFIM/Main_HTML/M_CL.html

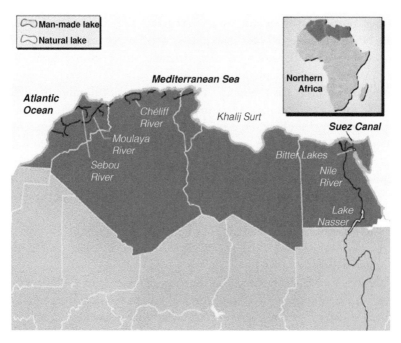

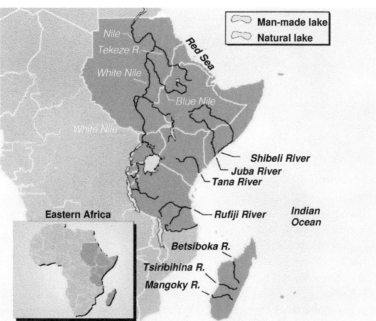

Figure 2.5 Africa: Hydrography of the five main regions

Note: See plate 8 for a colour version.

Source: www.courses.psu.edu/aaa_s/aaa_s110_tah/AFIM/Main_HTML/M_CL.html

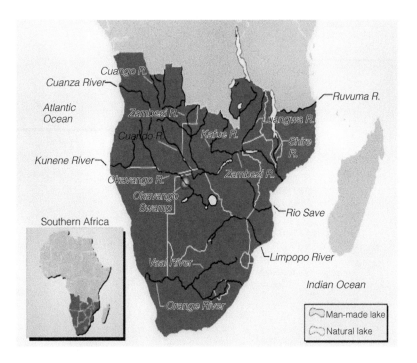

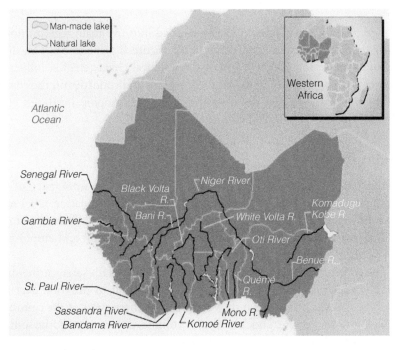

Figure 2.5 *Continued*

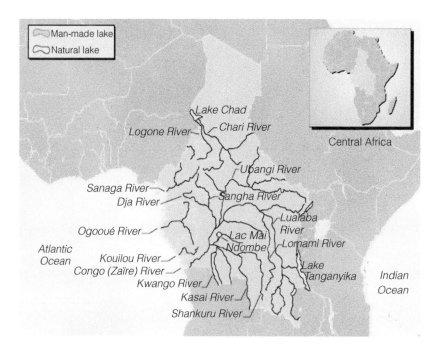

Figure 2.5 *Continued*

Hydrographically, the continent can be divided into five main regions: northern, eastern, southern, western and central (see Figure 2.5, plate 8). The different regional climates, together with the hydrographical characteristics, influence the degree of water availability in the different regions and countries on the continent.

The rest of the section discusses the specific geographical settings, climates and terrain in the 11 sampled countries in the study.

Burkina Faso[1]

Burkina Faso is a landlocked country in the north-western part of Africa covering about 274,000km². The country's estimated population is 13 million, with a growth rate of 2.5 per cent. Agriculture contributes about 40 per cent to the GDP (with livestock being a major agricultural activity) and employs about 90 per cent of the labour force.

The country has a dry tropical climate with two main seasons: the dry, and the rainy, which is generally from May to October but its duration decreases to only three months from the south-west to the northern parts of the country. The rainfall is also very erratic and, in terms of volume, decreases from the south-west to the north. The temperature experiences big seasonal variations and high ranges at night, particularly in the north of the country.

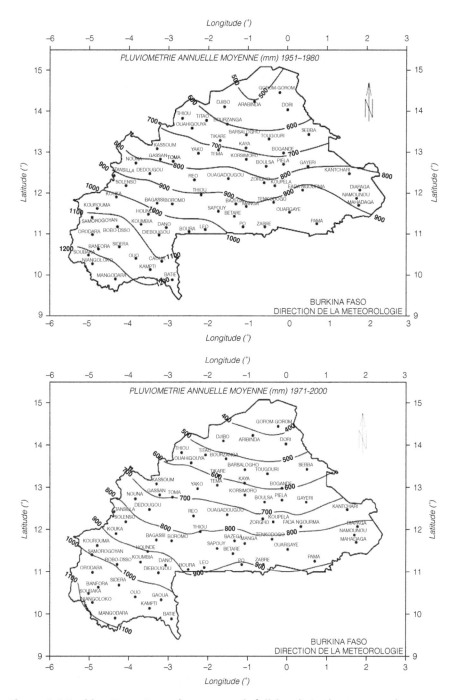

Figure 2.6 Burkina Faso: Annual average rainfall (mm). In the top panel are values for 1951–1980 and in the bottom panel are values for 1971–2000

Source: Ouedraogo et al (2006b)

The average annual precipitations for the 1951–1980 and 1971–2000 periods show even more significant variations as one moves from north to south (Figure 2.6). Significant changes in climate over time are seen as the isohyet's 1200mm disappears from Burkina Faso and the isohyet's 400mm is introduced in the north of the country in the second series.

The highest rainfall is experienced in August across the country. The rains cease from the end of September onwards. Figure 2.6 shows the average extreme rainfall from 1971 to 2000 in the capital Ouagadougou, similar to the rest of the country. The hydrographic network of Burkina Faso is quite dense, but most of the rivers are not permanent, which limits the availability of water and the possibilities of irrigation. The fertility of the soils is low with a limited water-holding capacity.

Cameroon[2]

Cameroon has a total land area of about 475,440km^2 and a coastline of 402km along the Gulf of Guinea. With a population of 17 million and a growth rate of 2 per cent, agriculture employs 70 per cent of the labour force and contributes 44 per cent to the GDP.

The country can be divided into three climate regions. Two clearly distinct climatic regions can be identified (Figure 2.7): the humid-wet-equatorial region in the south and a dry-semi-arid northern portion extending into the Sahel. In the humid region of the south annual rainfall often averages 1500mm and in the north an average rainfall of 500mm is recorded. The remainder of the country lies between these precipitation regimes, with distinct wet and dry seasons.

The south Cameroonian plateau and the coastal plain have a four-season equatorial climate, and forests. To the west, throughout a territory stretching from the mouth of the River Sanaga to the northern frontier of Northwest Province, the Guinean monsoon brings about a pseudo-tropical climate by the suppression of the short dry season which should occur in July–August. To the north, there is a two-season equatorial climate with a savanna showing some variations.

The country is characterized by high year-round temperatures and the weather is controlled by equatorial and tropical air masses. It has two major seasons, a dry and a wet season. Most of the rains in Cameroon fall between April and October, with rainfall highest at the coast but diminishing steadily northwards. Rainfall is variable and unreliable, and floods, frost, wind storms and droughts occur frequently in the country.

Temperatures decrease as both latitude and altitude increase. The southern Cameroon has an average temperature of about 25°C. In areas in the extreme north of the country, daily temperatures are very high, usually between 25°C and 34°C, with high amounts of sunshine. Two main factors influence temperature in Cameroon: the amount of cloud and rain, and the altitude.

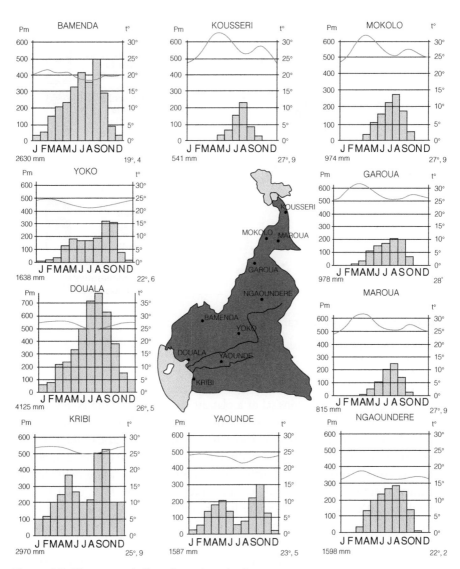

Figure 2.7 Climate and climatic regions in Cameroon

Source: Molua and Lambi (2006a)

Egypt[3]

Egypt lies in the north-eastern corner of Africa, with an area of about 1 million km². The population is estimated at 77 million, with a growth rate of 1.8 per cent, and with agriculture (with irrigation playing an important role) contributing 15 per cent to the GDP and employing 32 per cent of the labour force.

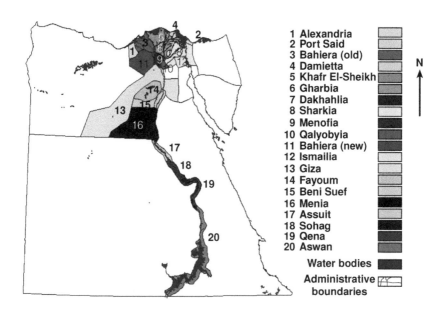

Figure 2.8 Egypt: Agricultural regions and Governorates

Note: See plate 9 for a colour version.
Source: Eid et al (2006)

The Egyptian terrain consists of a plateau interrupted by the Nile valley and delta. The inhabited area in the country does not exceed 3.5 per cent of the total area and it is confined to a narrow strip, which is the main course of the River Nile and agriculture from Aswan in the south to Cairo in the north (Figure 2.8, plate 9).

The country experiences north–south gradient temperature, with hot dry summers and mild winters. Yearly temperatures range from 19°C to 21°C in the Nile delta, 20°C to 22°C in Middle Egypt and 23°C to 27°C in South Egypt. Rain is low, irregular and unpredictable. The only region with meaningful rainfall is the northern coast, with 100–200mm/year. Within the delta, the precipitation is 40–60mm/year; precipitation in Middle Egypt is less than 20mm/year, whereas in the south and desert it does not exist.

Ethiopia[4]

Ethiopia is a landlocked country in the horn of Africa. It covers an area of 1.1 million km². The population is estimated at about 73 million, with a growth rate of 2.4 per cent, and 85 per cent of the population living in the rural areas. Agriculture (with the largest livestock population in Africa) contributes 40 per cent to the GDP and employs 80 per cent of the labour force (Alemayehu, 1998, 2003; CSA, 1998; Ministry of Agriculture (MoA), 2000).

Climatic elements, such as precipitation, temperature, humidity, sunshine, wind, are affected by geographic location and altitude. Ethiopia, being near the equator and with an extensive altitude range, has a wide range of climatic features suitable for different agricultural production systems. Taking the two extreme altitudes, temperatures range from the mean annual of 34.5°C in the Danakil Depression, while minimum temperatures fall below zero, with a mean of less than 0°C, in the upper reaches of Mount Ras Degen (4620m), where light snowfalls are recorded in most years. Between these extremes are vast areas of plateaux and marginal slopes where mean annual temperatures are between 10°C and 20°C.

Rainfall is also correlated with altitude (Figure 2.9, plate 10). Middle and higher altitudes (above 1500m) receive substantially greater falls than do the lowlands, except the lowlands in the west, where rainfall is high. Generally, average annual rainfall in areas above 1500m exceeds 900mm. In the lowlands (below 1500m) rainfall is erratic and averages below 600mm. There is strong inter-annual variability of rainfall all over the country. Despite variable rainfall, which makes agricultural planning difficult, a substantial proportion of the country gets enough rain for rainfed crop production (Alemayehu, 2003; FAO, 1984a and 1984b).

Natural vegetation of the country is influenced by five biomes: savanna, montane, tropical thickets, wooded steppe and desert. Agro-ecological zones in Ethiopia are traditionally classified into five categories with traditional names

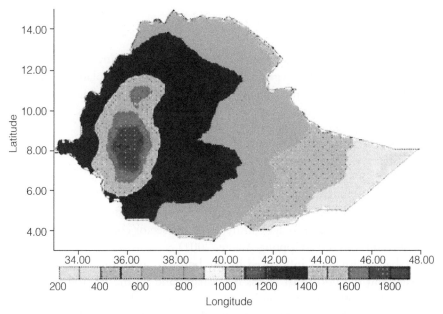

Figure 2.9 Ethiopia: Long-term average annual rainfall (mm/year)

Note: See plate 10 for a colour version.
Source: Alemayehu (2003)

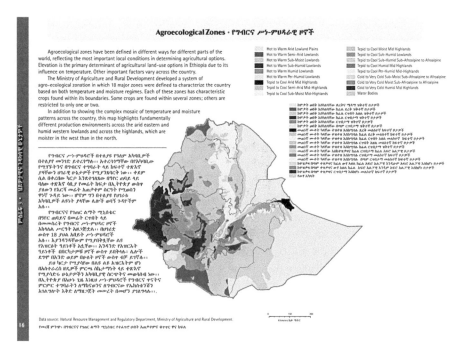

Figure 2.10 Ethiopia: Current major agroclimatic zones

Note: See plate 11 for a colour version.
Source: Deressa (2006)

assigned to each zone, based on altitude and temperature and also rainfall: bereha, kola, weinadega, dega and wurch (see Figure 2.10, plate 11). The wide ranges of topographic and climatic factors, parent material and land use have resulted in extreme variability of soils. About 19 soil types are identified throughout the country (MoA, 2000; Alemayehu, 2003).

Ghana

Ghana has a population of 18.4 million, with a growth rate of 2.5 per cent, and 68 per cent of the population living in the rural areas. About 52 per cent of the labour force is engaged in agriculture, with the sector contributing 54 per cent of the country's GDP (Oppong-Anane, 2001).

Ghana's climate is influenced by the hot, dry and dust-laden air mass that moves from the north-east across the Sahara, and by the tropical maritime air mass that moves from the south-west across the southern Atlantic ocean. The climate ranges from the bimodal rainfall equatorial type in the south to the tropical unimodal monsoon type in the north. The mean monthly temperature over most of the country never falls below 25°C, a consequence of the low-latitude position of Ghana and the absence of high-altitude areas. Mean annual temperature averages 27°C (Benneh et al, 1990; Oppong-Anane, 2001).

The rainfall generally decreases from the south to the north. The wettest area is the extreme south-west, where the rainfall is over 2000mm per annum. The driest area is in the south-eastern coastal tip, where the rainfall is about 750mm (Benneh et al, 1990; Oppong-Anane, 2001).

Ghana is divided into six major agro-ecological zones: rainforest, deciduous forest, forest-savanna transition, coastal savanna, plus northern (interior) savanna, which comprises Guinea and Sudan savannas. The rainfall determines largely the type of agricultural enterprise carried out in each zone.

Generally, most of Ghana's soils are plagued with inherent or human induced infertility. Interior savanna is low in organic matter (less than 2 per cent in the topsoil), has high levels of iron concretions and is susceptible to severe erosion. Thus, well-drained upland areas tend to be droughty and, when exposed to severe incident sun scorch, tend to develop cement-like plinthite. These conditions make it imperative that manure be incorporated regularly into the soils in the savanna zones (Ministry of Food and Agriculture (MoFA), 1998; Oppong-Anane, 2001).

Kenya[5]

Kenya has a land area of 580,367km^2. It has a population of 34 million, with a growth rate of 2.6 per cent. Agriculture contributes 16 per cent to the GDP and employs 75 per cent of the labour force (Kabubo-Mariara and Karanja, 2006; Orodho, 2001).

The country receives a bimodal type of rainfall where the 'long rains' fall between March and May while the 'short rains' fall between October and December. The average annual rainfall ranges from 250mm to 2500mm, with average potential evaporation from less than 1200mm to 2500mm, and the average annual temperature from less than 10°C to 30°C. All the mountain ranges have high rainfall, while it is dry tongues in the valleys and basins. The annual rainfall generally follows a strong seasonal pattern. The seasonal variations are strongest in the dry lowlands of the north and east, but weakest in the humid highlands of the central and Rift valley areas. Mean temperatures in Kenya are closely related to ground elevation (Kabubo-Mariara and Karanja, 2006).

In most parts of Kenya, soils are deficient in nitrogen (N), phosphorous (P) and occasionally potassium (K). In dry areas, the soils have low organic matter mainly because rainfall is low, variable, unreliable and poorly distributed. The country can be divided into three broad soil regions: humid, sub-humid and arid (Figure 2.11, plate 12). The sub-humid regions (Lake region and western Kenya) receive slightly less rainfall than the humid areas. The semi-arid regions (northern and north-eastern Kenya) receive on average 300–500mm of rainfall per year and the soils are shallow and generally infertile, but variable.

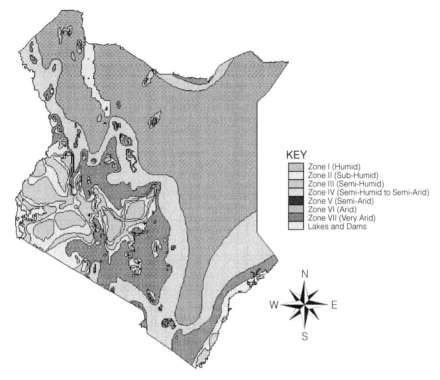

Figure 2.11 Kenya: Agroclimatic zones

Note: See plate 12 for a colour version.
Source: Sombroek et al (1982), cited in Kabubo-Mariara and Karanja (2006)

Niger[6]

Niger is a landlocked country in the Sahel. It has a total area of 1,267,000km^2, but only half of this is habitable due to adverse climatic or soil conditions. The country's population is estimated at 11 million, with a growth rate of 2.6 per cent. Agriculture contributes about 39 per cent to the GDP and employs 90 per cent of the labour force (Geesing and Djibo, 2001).

Niger has a mainly dry climate with considerable temperature variations. Potential evaporation is 2000–4000mm per annum, while rainfall nowhere exceeds 800mm and even falls to below 100mm over almost half the country. The rainfall pattern is Saharan in the north, with some 160mm falling in less than one month, except in the desert, where it practically never rains, and Sudano-Sahelian in the south, where some 600mm of rain falls during three to four months (June–September). Rainfall varies, however, from one region to another and its distribution is very erratic, with levels falling sharply as one moves northwards. Temperatures can exceed 40°C from March to June, the period of the 'harmattan'

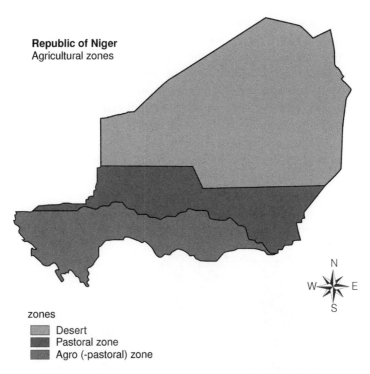

Republic of Niger
Agricultural zones

zones

Desert
Pastoral zone
Agro (-pastoral) zone

Figure 2.12 Niger: Agricultural zones and important livestock markets

Source: Geesing and Djibo (2001), cited in Maï Moussa and Amadou (2006)

wind. From November to February, temperatures drop considerably, particularly with nightfall. Annual temperature differences vary from around 16°C in the north-east to around 9°C in the south-west (Geesing and Djibo, 2001).

The vegetation of the country covers two geobotanical zones: the Saharo-Sindian in the very north and the major part, the Sudano-Zambezian zone. Biogeographically, Niger covers three areas: the Saharan, the Sahelian and the Sudanese (Figure 2.12). The transition between them is not clear-cut. The Saharo-Sindian zone in the north has little and very irregular, or sometimes no, rain. The dominant vegetation of the plains, if there is one, is a discontinuous grassland (often referred to as 'steppe') which is mostly limited to depressions. Plants have adapted to the absence of water (Geesing and Djibo, 2001).

Senegal[7]

Senegal is one of the Sahelian countries. It borders the Atlantic Ocean on the west with a coastline of more than 700km. The country has a population of 11 million, with a growth rate of 2.5 per cent. Agriculture contributes about 16 per cent to the GDP and employs between 60 and 77 per cent of the labour force (FAO, 2006; USAID, 2006).

Senegal is a relatively flat country, mostly rising to a maximum of 130m, though the south-east region has hills of up to 580m. Senegal's climate is affected by its position facing the Atlantic Ocean, and by atmospheric conditions determined by sea breeze and the harmattan (parching dusty land wind of the west African coast, occurring from December to February). There are two distinct seasons characterized by rainfall extremes: the dry season lasts from November to April; the rainy season lasts from May to October, beginning in the east and then spreading to the rest of the country. Precipitation decreases from 1500mm per year in the southern regions to 800mm in the central region

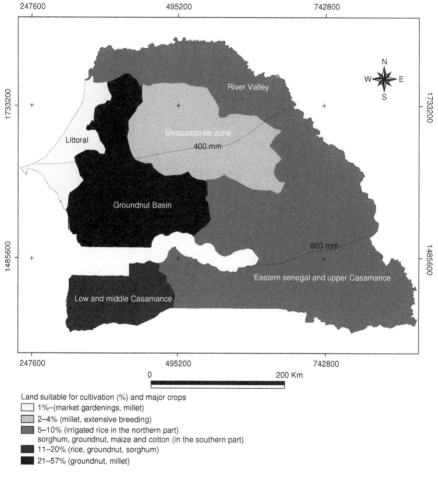

Figure 2.13 Agro-ecological zones in Senegal

Note: See plate 13 for a colour version.
Source: Pélissier (1983), cited in Sene et al (2006)

and then to 300mm in the north. The average annual temperature for the country is 28°C, with 27°C in the coastal areas and 35°C in the interior (FAO, 2006).

The vegetation of Senegal can be divided into three major ecological regions. From north to south, they are the Sahelian region, the Sudanian region, and the Guinean region, with several sub-divisions (Figure 2.13, plate 13) (USAID, 2006). The Sahelian region occurs between rainfall isohyets of 150mm and 700mm. The Sudanian region lies to the south of the Sahelian, covering about two-thirds of central and southern Senegal. It is the domain of the savanna. The typical vegetation types include the savanna woodland and the dry woodland. The region predominates between the 700mm and 1500mm isohyets and is centred on the 900mm to 1200mm isohyets. The Guinean region proper can only be found in the extreme south-west corner of Senegal, although characteristics of this zone begin to manifest themselves in the southern Sudanian region. This is the region of the semi-evergreen dense forest; its extent has been reduced to a few remnant communities by widespread deforestation for the cultivation of rice, manioc and peanuts. The Guinean region predominates in the areas of average annual rainfall exceeding 1500mm, with the central Guinean region having precipitation levels of over 1800mm. Despite the high rainfall, this region has a distinctly dry season of seven to eight months, distinguishing it from the Equatorial region of Africa (USAID, 2006).

South Africa[8]

South Africa is located at the southernmost tip of the African continent, with a coast stretching over 2500km. The country is bordered by the Atlantic Ocean on the west, the Indian Ocean on the south and east. The country's total land area is 1.2 million km^2 and its population is estimated at 46 million, with a current growth rate of less than 0.5 per cent. Agriculture contributes about 3.4 per cent to the GDP and employs 30 per cent of the labour force.

South Africa is located in a predominantly semi-arid part of the world. The climate varies from the desert and semi-desert in the dry north-west region to the sub-humid and wet along the eastern coastal area. The diverse agroclimatic zones allow for a huge diversity in terms of agricultural production. Four main climatic zones are identified in the country, namely, the desert, the arid (steppe), the subtropical and the subtropical wet (Poonyth et al, 2002).

With an average rainfall for the country of about 450mm per year, while evaporation is comparatively high, water is the most limiting factor in agricultural activities (Schulze et al, 2001). There is a wide regional variation in annual rainfall (Figure 2.14, plate 14). The rainfall decreases from east to west, from over 1000mm in the east to less than 100mm in the Namib and

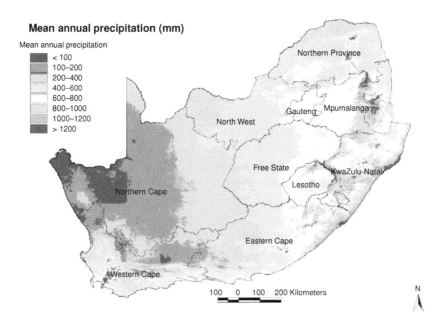

Figure 2.14 South Africa: Mean annual precipitation (mm)

Note: See plate 14 for a colour version.
Source: Schulze et al (2001), cited in Durand (2006)

Namaqualand desert regions. A 500mm rainfall line divides the country into two main sections, but three main rainfall regions could be identified in the country: the winter rainfall region in the south-western cape, with less than 500mm per year; the area along the southern coast, with rainfall throughout the year of more than 700mm; and the summer rainfall area in the rest of the country, with rainfall between 500mm and 700mm per year.

The weather in South Africa can be divided into two main seasons for farming activities: (i) summer season from October/November to March/April and (ii) winter season from April/May to August/September. Temperatures in summer vary on average across the country from 20°C to 35°C, and in winter from 6°C to 20°C. The temperatures are strongly determined by elevation and distance from the sea (Schulze, 1997; National Department of Agriculture (NDA), 2001a).

The soils in South Africa have been classified using a hierarchical system, and include a large number of soil bodies, ranging from black, *smectitic* clay on dolerite to yellow, *kaolinitic* clay on Beaufort sediments. The classification system contains two main levels, Soil Form and Soil Family. There are currently 73 soil forms, defined by the nature of the topsoil (organic, *humic, verti, melanic* or *othic*), and numerous diagnostic sub-soils horizons (Palmer and Ainslie, 2002).

Zambia[9]

Zambia is a landlocked country with a land area of 752,615km². The country's population is estimated at 11 million, with a growth rate of 2 per cent. Agriculture contributes an estimated 22 per cent to the GDP, employing 85 per cent of the labour force.

The country consists mostly of plateaux with an elevation from 950m to 1500m above sea level. The country has a subtropical climate and vegetation. There are three distinct seasons: a warm wet season stretching from November through April during which 95 per cent of the annual precipitation falls; a cool dry winter season from May to August with the mean temperature varying from 15°C to 27°C; and a hot dry season during September and October with an average maximum temperature of 27–32°C. The annual rainfall varies from over 1200mm in the north to about 700mm in the central part of the country and less than 700mm in the south.

Zambia is divided into three agro-ecological zones (Figure 2.15) with rainfall as the dominant climatic factor distinguishing the three zones.

There has been high variability in precipitation in Zambia in the last 30 years. However, the long-term mean annual rainfall isoquants do diminish from 1300mm per annum in the north-western part of the country to 700mm per annum in the southern part of the country (Figures 2.16).

Figure 2.15 Zambia: Agro-ecological zones

Note: Annual rainfall by region: I < 700mm; IIa 800–1000mm; IIb 800–1000mm; III 1000–1500mm.
Source: Jain (2006)

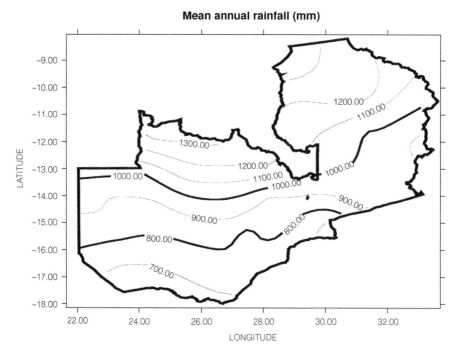

Figure 2.16 Zambia: Distribution of mean annual rainfall (mm)

Source: Jain (2006)

Zimbabwe[10]

Zimbabwe is a landlocked country in the southern African region with an area of 390,760km². The country's population is estimated at 12.7 million, with a growth rate of 0.51 per cent. Agriculture contributes 18 per cent to the GDP and employs 66 per cent of the labour force (Gambiza and Nyama, 2000; Mano and Nhemachena, 2006).

Three broad relief regions are generally recognized on the basis of elevation: the Lowveld (below 900m), the Middleveld (900–1200m) and the Highveld (1200–2000m). In addition, a narrow belt of mountains (2000–2400m), called the Eastern Highlands, runs north to south along the eastern border with Mozambique; and the deep cleft of the Zambezi river valley forms the boundary with Zambia in the north-west. Relief rainfall, increasing with altitude, largely influences climate. Mean annual rainfall varies from below 400mm in the extreme south of the Lowveld to above 2000mm on isolated mountain peaks in the eastern districts. Middleveld rainfall ranges from 500mm to 700mm and that of the Highveld from 800mm to 1000mm. Average annual temperature varies between 15°C in central regions of the

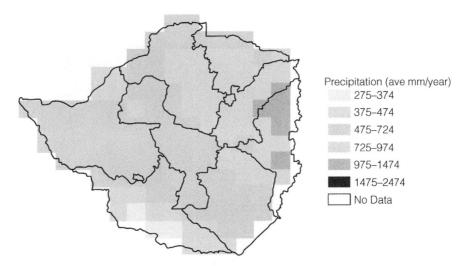

Figure 2.17a Zimbabwe: Spatial rainfall distribution

Note: See plate 15 for a colour version.
Source: Mano and Nhemachena (2006)

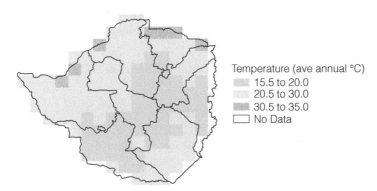

Figure 2.17b Zimbabwe: Spatial temperature distribution

Note: See plate 16 for a colour version.
Source: Mano and Nhemachena (2006)

country and 30°C in eastern and western regions of the country (Figures 2.17a and 2.17b, plates 15 and 16).

The country can be divided into five main ecological zones according to differences in effective rainfall (Figure 2.18, plate 17) (Gambiza and Nyama, 2000). The sandy, relatively infertile soils that cover some two-thirds of the country constitute the main soil type in the communal areas. Isolated areas of heavier more fertile soils occur throughout the country, the largest pockets being on the Highveld. Fertile irrigable basaltic *vertisols* occur extensively in the southern Lowveld.

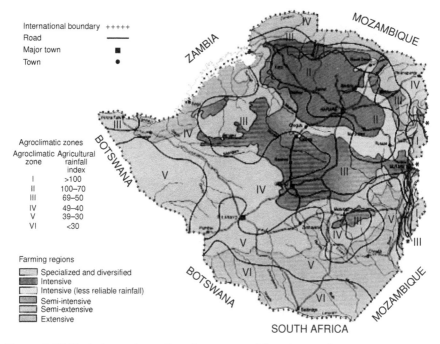

Figure 2.18 Zimbabwe: Agroclimatic zones and farming regions

Note: See plate 17 for a colour version.
Source: Gambiza and Nyama (2000), cited in Mano and Nhemachena (2006)

Notes

1.   Based on Ouedraogo et al (2006a) and Some et al (2006)
2.   Based on Molua and Lambi (2006a), (2006b)
3.   Based on Eid et al (2006)
4.   Based on Deressa (2006)
5.   Based on Kabubo-Mariara and Karanja (2006)
6.   Based in part on Maï Moussa and Amadou (2006)
7.   Based on Sene et al (2006)
8.   Based on Benhin (2006) and Durand (2006)
9.   Based on Jain (2006)
10. Based on Mano and Nhemachena (2006)

Methods and Models Developed and Used in the Study

The present study incorporated, modified and developed several methodologies during the course of the work. While the methodologies have been essential in conducting the analysis and interpreting the results, they are also important for work in other countries and continents. In this chapter we provide concise descriptions of these methodologies with detailed references for further details.

Cross sectional analysis

The cross sectional analysis is the cornerstone of this study. However, it has come a long way since its original publication (Mendelsohn et al, 1994). This section provides the modifications and updates made in the present study to the cross sectional analysis.

The Ricardian framework

The traditional Ricardian analysis examines farms across the landscape to reveal the differences in agricultural productivities in different climate zones (Mendelsohn et al, 1994). The farmer chooses the mix of species or crops to be grown and the inputs in order to maximize profits.[1] This analysis traces the locus of this maximum profit function over exogenous variables such as climate, soils, socio-economic variables and prices – important factors affecting farm net revenue that the farmer cannot control or alter. The model is estimated by regressing net revenue per hectare on a set of such variables. By comparing farmers' behaviour in different climate zones the Ricardian analysis estimates the likely long-run impact. The analysis controls for farm size, market access, soil type, topography and so on, but some future changes cannot be accounted for, such as new technologies in the future. The model also does not predict the consequences of future change in policies and institutions. This is still an issue to keep in mind when interpreting the results. The change in welfare resulting from a climate change is the predicted long-run change in net revenue per hectare. If the change increases net income, it is beneficial and if it decreases net income it is harmful to the farmer.

The Ricardian framework does not consider CO_2 impacts on crop production. (CO_2 concentrations are the same across climate zones, and the Ricardian approach cannot, therefore, detect the impact of CO_2.) Global warming will be associated with increased concentrations of CO_2 that are expected to be beneficial to crop production. A modification to the Crop Water (CROPWAT) model (Food and Agriculture Organization (FAO), 1993) that takes into account the CO_2 effect is presented and applied in a following section of this chapter (see 'Use of models').

There are two important issues that must be addressed in applying this model to small-scale farmers. First, households use their own labour and there is no observed wage for self employed household labour. In the absence of household wages, we do not treat household labour as a paid input.[2] Second, households often consume a large fraction of their output. In this study, we value own consumption of farm output at the prevailing market prices and add it to the farm income.

The model is precise in the vicinity of the sample data, for example, valuing marginal changes in developing countries. However, if climate changes a great deal and this leads to a dramatic change in the output or input quantities, prices will likely change (Cline, 1996). The Ricardian model will overstate welfare changes if there are large price changes. That is, price changes will modify the welfare impacts predicted by the model. A more detailed explanation of the modifications made to the Ricardian approach at the regional level in the study in Africa can be found in Kurukulasuriya and Mendelsohn (2006a), Seo and Mendelsohn (2006a) and Maddison et al (2006); at the country level they can be found in Mano and Nhemachena (2006), Kabubo-Mariara and Karanja (2006) and Benhin (2006).

Farmer choice analysis

Although the Ricardian model provides an estimate of the impacts of climate change given farmer adaptation, it does not reveal how farmers actually adapt to climate change. Different farmers in different locations, under different environmental and socio-economic conditions, may respond differently to climate change. We developed a household decision-making model that allows us to incorporate micro-level considerations into our Ricardian analysis. We therefore conducted a second set of analyses that explicitly examines whether farmers' decisions are sensitive to climate. We explicitly modelled the farmers' decision whether to manage livestock, the choice of livestock species, the number of livestock to own, which crops to grow and the choice of irrigation.

For all of these choices, we assume that farmers maximize net revenue. We then used discrete choice models for yes and no decisions (such as irrigation or no irrigation) and multinomial models for choices across many alternatives (such as raising beef cattle, milk cattle, sheep, poultry or goats). In each case, we regressed the choice on prices, climate, soils, region of Africa and a few other control variables (Kurukulasuria and Mendelsohn, 2006a, 2006b; Seo and Mendelsohn, 2006c).

Structural Ricardian analysis

The Structural Ricardian model combines the adaptations by farmers with the net revenue modelling of the Ricardian technique in a sequenced way. Instead of estimating the net revenue function across all choices (such as in the Ricardian method), the Structural Ricardian model first decides what choices a farmer makes and then estimates the net revenue function for that specific choice. For example, a farmer will first choose beef cattle or sheep and then look at the net revenue function of beef cattle and the net revenue function of sheep. The net revenue function reveals the underlying response of each output to climate, soils and other control variables. Combined with the choice model of each farmer, one can find how farmers react to climate change and what will happen to net revenue.

The optimization decision of a farmer can be seen as a simultaneous multiple-stage procedure; in this study it was applied to livestock decisions (Seo and Mendelsohn 2006b). The farmer chooses the levels of inputs, the desired number of animals, and the species that would yield the highest net profit. Given the profit maximizing set and level of inputs for each farmer, one can estimate the loci of profit maximizing choices for each animal across exogenous environmental factors such as temperature or precipitation. These are the individual loci that lie beneath the overall profit function for the farm

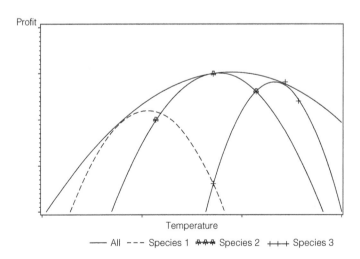

Figure 3.1 Theoretical livestock response functions

Source: Seo and Mendelsohn (2006b)

(Mendelsohn et al, 1994). For example, in Figure 3.1 we display a traditional Ricardian response function with respect to temperature. Underneath the loci of all choices is a set of animal-specific response functions. The farmer must choose which animal will give him the most profit and then which inputs will maximize the value of that animal given the temperature. We examine the individual response functions (Structural Ricardian model) as well as the overall response function (Ricardian model). The change in welfare from a non-marginal change in climate is the change in expected net revenue. It depends on the change for each species and whether the farmer switches from one species to another.

Impact

The economic impact of climate change on farmers in Africa was estimated using climate sensitivity surface estimates (from the Ricardian analysis) and predicted climate change ranges in a given future. The results from the Ricardian analysis provided the marginal change in welfare (net revenue per hectare) resulting from a marginal change in climate (precipitation and temperature). When these values are entered into a set of future predicted temperatures and precipitation values one can estimate the range of impacts of climate change on African farmers. In order to extrapolate from the 11 countries in the study sample to the entire continent we had to use data on the distribution of crop land, irrigated and rainfed, across Africa.

Two types of climate scenarios were considered: uniform and general circulation model. The first type assumed a uniform change (within the range of predicted climate change by 2020, 2060 and 2100) across Africa. While simplistic in assuming uniform change across the continent, it served our purpose of comparing relative vulnerability in the various countries in our study. The second type used three scenarios consistent with the range of outcomes in the most recent Intergovernmental Panel on Climate Change (IPCC) report (Houghton et al, 2001). The study employed three atmospheric-oceanic global circulation models (AOGCMs) namely Canadian Climate Centre (CCC) (Boer et al, 2000), Centre for Climate System Research (CCSR) (Emori et al, 1999), and Parallel Climate Model (PCM) (Washington et al, 2000) to provide grid-level predicted climate by 2020, 2060 and 2100. In each of these scenarios, climate changes at the grid cell level were summed to predict average climate changes by country. We then examined the consequences of these country-level climate change scenarios for 2020, 2060 and 2100.

Adaptation

Adaptation was analysed, using several approaches. A special section of the survey instrument (see below) included specific questions about adaptation. The analysis explored how farmers in each location adopted different management practices, cropping, and livestock varieties to maximize profit given the climate they currently faced. The relationship between adoption and climate was then used to analyse how adoption would change with climate change. This section first reviews some economic aspects of adaptation to climate change. (An African-focused review of more technical-agronomic aspects can be found in Annex 1.) The literature suggested several behavioural and institutional links that were incorporated into the various reported analyses.

Perception of climate change, adaptation practices and barriers

The survey instrument that was presented earlier (also in Annex 2) also includes a segment that recorded information relating to the perception of climate change, the adaptations farmers state they have made, and their perception of barriers to adaptation. In a special set of questions farmers were requested to describe verbally any observed long-term changes in temperature and precipitation, as well as any measures that they had taken in order to adapt to whatever changes they had seen. Finally they were asked what the greatest obstacles to adaptation were.

The answers to these questions were subsequently coded as discrete variables following discussion with the country teams responsible for implementing the survey. Responses to the question on whether the farmer had witnessed changes in temperature were classified as falling into one or more of six different categories: 'warmer', 'cooler', 'more extreme', 'other', 'no change' and 'don't know'. The question on whether the farmer had witnessed changes in precipitation was classified as falling into one of seven different categories: 'increased', 'decreased', 'change in timings of rains', 'change in frequency of droughts', 'other changes in precipitation' and 'no change in precipitation'. Nearly 25 different categories were identified for adaptations to climate change and 12 different barriers to climate change were identified.

Adaptation to climate change requires that farmers using traditional techniques of agricultural production first notice that the climate has altered. Farmers then need to identify potentially useful adaptations and then implement them. The analysis of the adaptation data addressed specifically the following questions (Maddison et al, 2006):

- Do farmers perceive climate change to have occurred already and if so, have they begun to adapt?
- What kinds of adaptations have been made to climate change?
- What kind of farmers do fail to respond?
- What if any is the role of government in overcoming barriers to adaptation?

The results of these analyses are presented in Chapter 5.

Estimates of endogenous adaptation in crops and livestock
In addition to exploring climate change perceptions and stated adaptations, the analysis also explores the actual behaviour of farmers across different climate zones. This analysis quantifies the changes that farmers have made from place to place to adapt to the climate they face. It quantifies who has adapted and who has not and how. The analysis of adaptation decisions is based on the principles of the adoption of technology literature, which will not be reviewed here. Using the data that was collected in Africa, several analyses were performed on livestock and crop choices and the choice of irrigation in Africa (Kurukulasuriya and Mendelsohn, 2006a, 2006b; Seo and Mendelsohn, 2006c). Farmers managing both small and large farms in Africa do consider changing their practices and such decisions are a function of climate, human capital, existing institutions and the physical characteristics of the farm.

Data collection and generation

The study, an empirical investigation, relied very heavily on data. Significant efforts were made to obtain the best and most reliable data, as is explained in the following sections.

Hydrological data

Data concerning the hydrology was obtained by a team comprising of the University of Colorado and the International Water Management Institute (IWMI) (Strzepek and McCluskey, 2006). Using a hydrological model for Africa and actual data in various locations, the hydrology team calculated flow and runoff for each district in the surveyed countries and each province in Africa and calibrated the model results to the existing observations. Figure 3.2 (Plate 18) depicts the distribution of estimated baseline flow (in millions m^3/yr) across the continent (Kurukulasuriya and Mendelsohn, 2006c). Data on elevation at the centroid of each district is obtained from the United States Geological Survey (USGS, 2004). The USGS data is derived from a global digital elevation model (DEM) with a horizontal grid spacing of 30 arc seconds (approximately 1km). For more explanation see Strzepek and McCluskey (2006).

ARTES (for precipitation)

The precipitation data comes from the Africa Rainfall and Temperature Evaluation System (ARTES) (World Bank, 2003). This dataset, created by the National Oceanic and Atmospheric Association's Climate Prediction Center, is based on interpolations across ground station measurements of precipitation

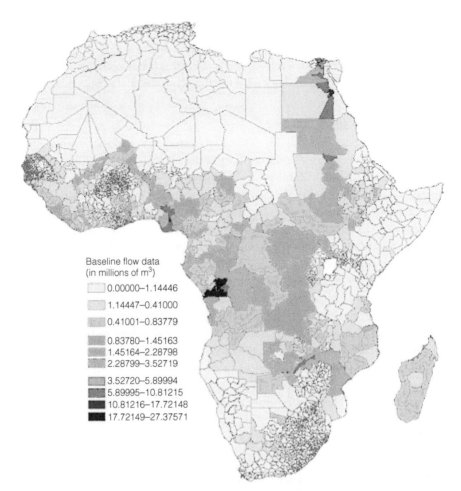

Baseline flow data
(in millions of m³)

0.00000–1.14446
1.14447–0.41000
0.41001–0.83779
0.83780–1.45163
1.45164–2.28798
2.28799–3.52719
3.52720–5.89994
5.89995–10.81215
10.81216–17.72148
17.72149–27.37571

Figure 3.2 Africa: Baseline flow data (million cubic metres)

Note: See plate 18 for a colour version.
Source: Kurukulasuriya and Mendelsohn (2006c)

across Africa, which were assigned to grids of 0.5 by 0.5 degrees across the entire African continent. The data spans the period 1947 to 2003.

Satellite data (for temperature)

The temperature data comes from satellites operated by the US Department of Defense (Basist et al, 2001). The Defense Department uses a set of polar orbiting satellites that pass over the entire earth at 6am and 6pm every day. The satellites are equipped with sensors that detect microwaves that can pass through clouds and detect surface temperature (Weng and Grody, 1998) across the entire planet. For more details see Mendelsohn et al (2007).

Economic household data

The economic data is based on a questionnaire that was administered in the various sample districts in each country. The following sections provide the information on the methodology used for the economic data collection.

Farmers' sample survey design

The economic data for this study was collected, by national teams, in 11 countries: Burkina Faso, Cameroon, Ethiopia, Egypt, Kenya, Ghana, Niger, Senegal, South Africa, Zambia and Zimbabwe. The countries themselves represent a diversity of climates across Africa. Further, in each country, districts were chosen to get a wide representation of farms across climate conditions in that country (Table 3.1). In each chosen district, a survey instrument was conducted of randomly selected farms. The sampling was clustered in villages to reduce sampling costs.

A total of 9598 surveys was administered across the 11 countries in the study. The number of surveys across countries varied. Not all the surveys could be used. Some observations had missing data and some answers were erratic. Impossible values were removed from the sample and judged to be missing. It is not clear what the sources of these errors were but field and measurement errors are most likely. They may reflect a misunderstanding of the units of measurement, they may reflect a language barrier, or they may be intentional incorrect answers. The final number of useable surveys is 9064.

Table 3.1 *Africa: Summary of districts in each country*

Country	Area (km²)	Number of districts	Nos. of districts selected by country teams	Observations	Useable observations
Burkina Faso	273,719	301	50	1087	1031
Cameroon	466,307	58	50	801	751
Egypt	982,910	27	18	900	802
Ethiopia	1,132,328	65	50	998	940
Ghana	239,981	110	60	894	878
Kenya	584,429	48	38	816	754
Niger	1,186,021	36	30	900	897
Senegal	196,911	320	72	1078	1068
South Africa	1,221,943	372	17	416	286
Zambia	754,773	72	61	1008	970
Zimbabwe	390,804	60	22	700	687
Total	7,430,126	1469	468	9598	9064

Survey instrument

A survey instrument designed for this study covers a detailed description of the crops and livestock grown and sold by each farmer and for how much, the costs of farming, household and farm characteristics, and select information about extension, adaptation and market access (Annex 2). The survey was designed by team members and then tested in the field. Based on initial responses, the survey was shortened and modified.

The instrument attempted to capture information on pertinent variables required to calculate net farm revenues, as well as to explain the variations in net farm revenues, land values and income across representative sample districts, and agroclimatic regions in the respective countries. The period of interest were the 2002/2003 (for Burkina Faso, Egypt, Ghana, Niger, Senegal, South Africa and Zambia) and the 2003/2004 (for Cameroon, Ethiopia, Kenya and Zimbabwe) farming seasons.

In addition to asking farmers what they did in the prior season, the questionnaire also asked about farmers' knowledge, attitudes and perception of climate variation and climate change. The questionnaire had two main parts and seven sections. Part 1 focused mainly on crop production while part 2 was on livestock production activities. Sections 1 and 2 focused on household characteristics and employment of the household head. The questions in section 3 collected information on the household's land under farming activities (both crops and livestock), and farm labour used for different farm activities and respective costs. In section 4, detailed information was obtained on crop farming activities with respect to the type of crops grown, the size of land planted, amount harvested and sold, and other crop farming related costs such as seeds, fertilizer and pesticides, light and heavy machinery and animal power, and farming related buildings. Parts of section 4 requested information on the type of livestock, poultry and other animals farmed, how many were purchased, lost and sold in the period of interest. It also required similar information on livestock and poultry products, such as milk, beef, eggs and wool. In section 5, the focus was on access to information for farming activities and the sources and cost of these information items. Section 6 asked questions concerning the total income of the farm household (for both farming and non-farming activities), taxes paid and subsidies received in the period of interest. And finally, section 7 consisted of eliciting information from farmers on their perception about short- and long-term climate change and their adaptation strategies in response to these perceived climate variations and climate changes.

The survey concentrated on farm households in the predominant farm types in each district/province. An effort was made to survey both small and large farms. The typology of representative farm types for each district was established by country teams to capture key features of agricultural production activities such as scale (reflecting technology), cropping systems and land tenure regimes, among others. The country-level sample design followed these procedures:

- The number of collection units (districts/province) were within the range of 17–70.
- Aggregation/disaggregation of sampling units was guided by a gradient of climate attributes (i.e. significant change in temperature).
- Within each survey unit, a minimum of two and a maximum of five farm types were surveyed.
- The survey of farming activities within each farm type targeted the typical farm households in the selected category, with a sample in the range of 5–10 households for each farm type in each district.
- The sample sizes had a trade-off between the number of households and number of districts – more households and less districts on one hand, and less households and more districts on the other – with a sample size for each country in the range of 400–1100. The total number of households surveyed in each country and the number of observations actually used after verification of the data can be found in Table 3.1.

Soils data

Soils data were obtained for each district from FAO (2003). The FAO data provide information about the major and minor soils in each location as well as slope and texture. The FAO classifies soils into 26 major units and several sub-categories based on soil texture (coarse, medium or fine) and the slope of the land. Three slope classes are distinguished: (a) level to gently undulating, with generally less than 8 per cent slope; (b) rolling to hilly with slopes from 8 to 30 per cent; and (c) steeply dissected to mountainous, with more than 30 per cent slope. The major soil types are: *Acrisols, Cambisols, Chernozems, Podzoluvisols, Rendzinas, Ferrasols, Gleysols, Phaeozems, Lithosols, Fluvisols, Kastanozems, Luvisols, Greyzems, Nitosols, Histosols, Podzols, Arenosols, Regosols, Solonetz, Andosols, Rankers, Vertisols, Planosols, Xerosols, Yermosols, Solonchaks* (FAO, 2003).

The sub-categories are indicated by the symbol of the dominant soil unit, followed by a number which refers to the descriptive legend. For example, associations where *lithosols* are dominant are marked by the *lithosol* symbol *I* combined with one or two association soil units or inclusions, and where there are no associated soils, the symbol *I* alone is used. When information on the texture of the surface layers (upper 30cm) of the dominant soil is available, a texture class (1, 2, 3) follows the association symbol, separated from it by a dash. Where two or three groups of textures occur that could be separated, two or three figures may be used, separated by a slash. Slope classes are indicated by a small (lower case) letter: *a, b* or *c*, immediately following the texture notation (FAO, 2003).

Use of models

Several models were also developed and or adapted for use in the study. The FAO CROPWAT model played a major role in benchmarking the results of the Ricardian analysis in the various countries.

CROPWAT[3]

While the cross sectional approach that was suggested for studying the likely impact of climate change on African agriculture has been in use for quite some time and it is quite robust and trustworthy, it was felt during the project design stages that a benchmark analysis was needed as well. A benchmark analysis can be of various natures and level of complications. To best address the need for benchmark analysis, it was agreed that a crop modelling approach that is already in use in the African region, and that is familiar to the country team members, and would not need complicated software, would be used. It was also agreed that the approach to be selected should be, as much as possible, easy on data and should not engage extensive data collection efforts. The CROPWAT software was selected and used by the country teams. The methodology behind CROPWAT was developed by the Land and Water Division of FAO (FAO, 1993). Its main functions are to calculate reference evapotranspiration, crop water requirements and crop irrigation requirements in order to develop irrigation schedules under various management conditions and scheme water supply, and to evaluate rainfed production, drought effects and efficiency of irrigation practices. The methodology was further modified during the present Global Environment Facility (GEF) project in Africa to study crop water requirements as affected by climate change.

This analysis was conducted in two phases. In the first phase of the study, five crops – beans, groundnuts, maize, millet and sorghum – were selected for two districts in each country for the analysis of climate change impacts on present crop water use. (A couple of countries analysed more crops and in more than two districts.) In the second phase, the countries used climate change scenarios to forecast future changes in water requirement of these crops.

The main characteristics of the farming system in the project countries and their vulnerability include:

- **Agro-pastoral millet/sorghum**. Rainfed sorghum and pearl millet are the main sources of food and are rarely marketed, whereas sesame and pulses are sometimes sold. Livestock is kept for subsistence and transportation. The main source of vulnerability is drought, leading to crop failure, weak animals and distress sale of assets.
- **Irrigated**. Large and small irrigation schemes with high population density and small farm size. Crop failure is generally not a problem but livelihoods are vulnerable to water shortages.

- **Cereal root cropped mixed**. Cereals, such as maize, millet and sorghum, are widespread. Intercropping is common. This farming system is predominantly in the dry sub-humid zone. Livestock is abundant. Main source of vulnerability is drought.
- **Large commercial and small holder**. Located mainly in semi-arid and dry sub-humid zone of South Africa and Namibia. It comprised two distinctive types of farms: scattered smallholder farms and large commercialized farms. Both types are largely mixed cereals/livestock systems. Small farmers often survive by means of off-farm income from employment. Poor soils and drought are the sources of vulnerability.
- **Maize mixed**. This farming system lies mainly in east and southern Africa in altitudes of 800m to 1500m. It also contains scattered small-scale irrigation schemes. Climate varies from dry sub-humid to moist sub-humid. The main staple is maize and the main cash sources are sales from food crops like maize and pulses, migrant remittances, cattle, small ruminants, tobacco and coffee.
- **Pastoral**. Mainly based on sheep, goats and camels, this system is largely located in the arid and semi-arid zones. The main source of vulnerability is great climatic variability and consequently high incidence of drought.

Actual water use of the selected five crops was assessed using FAO methodology outlined in Irrigation and Drainage Papers 33 (Doorenbos and Kassam, 1977) and 56 (Allen et al, 1998) and CROPWAT programme (FAO, 1993).

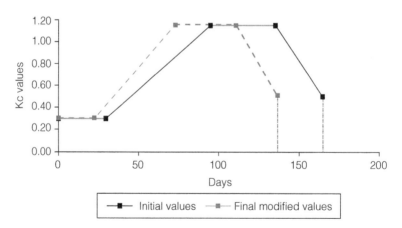

Figure 3.3 Impact of increased temperature and CO_2 concentration level on crop growth stages

Note: Kc is a dimensionless coefficient that measures water use consumption of a given crop in comparison to a reference crop.
Source: Wahaj et al (2006)

CROPWAT was also modified (to Crop Water with Climate Change (CROPWATCC)) so it can be used to assess the changes in the length of crop growth stages in response to climate change via changes in average temperature and CO_2 concentration in the atmosphere (Wahaj et al, 2006). These 'new' values of the length of crop growth stages can then be used with the climate data generated by general circulation models (GCM) to compute 'future' crop water requirements. The methodology is described in Wahaj et al (2006). A description of the combined impact of temperature and CO_2 on length of the growing period is presented in Figure 3.3.

Hydrological model[4]

One of the most significant impacts of climate change is likely to be on the hydrological system, and hence on river flows and regional water resources. This will be particularly true in arid and semi-arid areas of Africa, where water resources are very sensitive to climate variability, particularly rainfall. Because farmer behaviour is particularly affected by availability of water, and because information on runoff and flows are not readily available in Africa, there was a need to (a) develop an approach that enables flow and runoff to be derived for the districts of interest; (b) develop time series (1961–1990) of runoff and flow for the districts that will provide a baseline for climate change scenarios; and (c) provide hydrologically relevant parameters that can be used as independent variables in the Ricardian analyses.

The contribution of a continent-wide hydrological model rather than a catchment or water resource system level model is that it allows the use of runoff and flow estimates in any part of the country (some will have zero values obviously). The model inputs were the climate variables of the 1961–1990 climatology and physiological parameters (e.g. soil properties and land use) derived from global datasets for each of the 0.5° latitude/longitude cells across the continent. The primary model output comprised a time series (monthly time step) of simulated runoff for all the grid cells. For each of the districts in the study countries the runoff was computed as the area weighted average of the runoff generated on all the cells that lay within that district. When a district lay entirely within a cell the runoff was assumed to be the same as that across the cell. No attempt was made to disaggregate data within cells. The runoff was also accumulated and 'routed' via a drainage network to simulate flow. This enabled flow into and out of each district to be estimated. The model used is a version of a conceptual rainfall-runoff model called Water Balance (WATBAL) (Yates, 1997), which can be applied to gridded data. The model simulates changes in soil moisture and runoff, taking into account water inflows and outflows from surface and subsurface, precipitation and evapotranspiration (land cover). The hydrological model predicted 'potential' flow and did not take into account actual current uses of water.

The model was calibrated against observed flow data (i.e. discharge from gauging stations) and land use, obtained from some country teams and with additional data obtained from the Flow Regimes from International Experiments and Network Data (FRIEND) database. Consequently, another calibration was made against an existing runoff dataset. These were developed by the University of New Hampshire (UNH) and the Global Runoff Data Center (GRDC).

Once calibrated, the model was run to estimate runoff, on a monthly time step, for all grid cells for the period 1961–1990, and also to calculate flow by having runoff from each grid cell accumulated along the drainage network and providing the stream flow in each grid cell. Additional indexes were calculated, such as the river density index and the percentage of area irrigated in each cell. Given that the Ricardian economic analysis uses flow and runoff as well as area irrigated by cells, the results of this model are very useful for the economic analysis that was constructed on both country and regional levels.

Notes

1. This is equivalent to saying that farmers seek to maximize benefits.
2. This might lead to biased results if off-farm wages (opportunity cost of time) are correlated with climate.
3. Based on Wahaj et al (2006).
4. Based on Strzepek and McCluskey (2006).

4

Results of the Country Analyses

This chapter provides country-level results from the various analyses that have been conducted in the study. We present first the agronomic results based on the Crop Water (CROPWAT) and the Crop Water with Climate Change (CROPWATCC) (in South Africa only) applications.[1] These are followed by the economic impact analyses by country. This chapter is not meant to be conclusive in that it presents only a short description of the applications in the various countries, and indicative results. The interested reader is referred to the country studies that are referenced in the sources for each reported analysis.

Analysis of impacts on crop water requirements

CROPWAT simulations were conducted for each country in the study and for main crops that have been identified and agreed upon by the country team members. The country simulation was conducted in three to five of the sampled study regions in each country. (Some countries included all sampled regions in their simulations.) The usefulness of the CROPWAT analysis can be seen in Table 4.1, where parameters for maize in different countries are calculated and compared, and a total water use for the area under cultivation is estimated.

The results in Table 4.1 indicate the wide variation in both the crop water use and the yield per unit of land and water. Having such variation across the continent explains the differences in area under maize in the different countries. More important, use of such information could be critical in policy decisions at the regional level. Having relative advantages for certain crops in certain countries or regions within a country could be taken into account in a supra-continent accord for specialization and allocation of crop production quotas across countries. We will get back to this point in the policy discussion at the end of the chapter.

While the inclusion of all country results will be impossible due to the large size and number of the individual country tables, it is useful to provide the conclusion reached in each simulation. A synthesis of these conclusions will be provided below.

Table 4.1 *Actual crop water use and yields for maize in various districts of project countries*

Country	District	ETo (mm)	ETm (mm)	Ky	Ya (t/ha)	Ym (t/ha)	Ks	Cropped area (ha)	ETa (mm)	Crop water use (MCM)
Burkina Faso	Bobo-Dioulasso	596	480	1.25	1.4	4.0	0.48	61,430	230	142
	Fada N' Gourma	633	512	1.25	0.8	3.0	0.41	13,750	212	29
Egypt	Khafr El-Shiekh	678	557	1.25	9	9	0.00	32,132	549	176
Ethiopia	Adama	563	532	1.25	2.3	3.5	0.72	na	257	na
	Miesso	426	375	1.25	1.4	3.5	0.53	na	197	na
Senegal	Kolda	637	389	1.25	0.8	1.2	0.80	31,490	312	98
South Africa	Kroonstad	759	575	1.25	0.79	7	0.29	88,805	167	148
	Lichtenburg	624	484	1.25	0.70	7	0.28	239,750	136	325
	Middelburg	740	581	1.25	2.40	7	0.47	130,718	276	360

Note: ETo = potential or reference evapotranspiration; ETm = maximum crop evapotranspiration; Ky = yield response factor; Ya = actual yield; Ym = maximum achievable yield; Ks = water stress coefficient; ETa = actual crop evapotranspiration or actual crop water use; MCM = million cubic metre; t/ha = tonnes per hectare.

Source: Wahaj et al (2006)

Burkina Faso[2]

A rainfall (reduction) trend with implications for crop production and food security has been detected and evaluated in Burkina Faso. Six provinces out of 45 were selected for the CROPWAT simulations: Houet (Bobo-Dioulasso), Poni (Gaoua), Gourma (Fada N'Gourma), Kadiogo (Ouagadougou), Yatenga (Ouahigouya) and Seno (Dori). The simulations analysed the way differences between the six provinces and between crops are related to climate variables. This hinges on the premise that weather variability and uneven distributions of precipitation strongly influence crop yield.

The main outcome of these simulations shows that soil water reserves naturally increase according to rainfall. But in general the soil's water-holding capacity is low in Burkina Faso. In the southern part of the country, water requirements for cereal crops and groundnut are met by the rainfall. In the Sudano-Sahelian and Sahelian regions, water deficits are experienced towards the end of the rainy season. Supplementary irrigation is needed to enable cereal crops to finish their cycle normally. In the cotton belt, irrigation needs for cotton and maize are very low, but in the centre, the north and the Sahel, irrigation needs at the end of the season are substantial.

Cameroon[3]

Because physical conditions in Cameroon vary, cropping systems and types of crop cultivated vary throughout the country. Three agro-ecologies were thus sampled for comparative analysis: Ambam in the humid moist forest zone; Bamenda in the high savanna zone; and Garoua in the Sahel savanna zone. From the crop water simulation, three major crops were identified for analysis – maize, groundnuts and soybean.

The findings of the simulations in Cameroon indicate that even though farmers may be adapting to the climatic variation, the government needs to help the adaptation process by making available the necessary resources and providing irrigation infrastructure, especially in the drier northern parts of the country, to counter the debilitating effect of low soil moisture, peaking daily temperatures and runaway evapotranspiration. To ease water constraints and enhance productivity, there is a need to modify cropping patterns and cultivate crops with lower water requirements, and improve irrigation by changing the traditional system to more efficient systems such as drip irrigation and pipe irrigation. Crop water demand must be met as this strongly determines crop emergence, development and survival in the tropical regions.

Egypt[4]

Wheat, maize and cotton were selected for the study since they represent different growing seasons and water needs. The evaluation was carried out in the three main agricultural regions of Egypt: the delta (lower Egypt), represented by the Kafr El-Sheikh governorate; middle Egypt, represented by the Giza governorate; and upper Egypt represented by the Sohag governorate. According to the study, the effect of climate warming on the water use of wheat, maize and cotton increased in the three selected locations. At the same time, increasing temperature under climate change simulations caused some yield reduction, particularly at the third growth stage with the summer crops (maize and cotton).

Climate change could therefore increase crop water use and reduce yields. Strategies for adapting to climate change may involve the development of new, more heat-tolerant cultivars, and new crops (more cotton cultivation as an alternative to some maize and more winter legumes instead of some wheat). Changing the cotton crop practices (optimum sowing date, cultivars, water amount and plant density) could allow farmers to benefit from new varieties or technologies. Further adaptation may modify the cropping pattern (e.g. partly growing cotton after wheat in the same year and on the same land); reducing or retaining the current area under cultivation for some high water consumer crops (e.g. sugar cane and rice); and changing practices (using optimum sowing dates, more water, more nitrogen, and suitable cultivars for the particular agroclimatological region).

Ethiopia[5]

CROPWAT was used to simulate yield responses and crop water use for maize and sorghum crops in two districts of Ethiopia – Adama and Miesso. The results showed that the water used by crops in both these districts was far less than actually needed, with pronounced effects on the simulated yield reduction percentage. The results show a decrease in yield of 40–70 per cent as a result of the increase in evaporation rate. Increased evaporation because of higher temperatures combined with the reduction in rainfall and lower water availability in the soil means that the supply of water does not match the needs. This affects the overall condition of plants and their yield.

Various adaptive measures can be considered and are practised in these districts as well as all over the country. Some of these adaptive measures are: using supplementary irrigation such as small irrigation and water harvesting; minimizing evaporative demand by using mulch; and applying soil moisture conservation techniques and crop management practices that reduce sensitivity to water stress. Most of these adaptive measures are undertaken at farm level. This depends on farmers' perception of water stress conditions. In the two districts studied, farmers are adjusting planting density and the timing of various operations, and using conservation tillage and intercropping. They are also introducing traditional irrigation and water harvesting methods to cope with the water stress problem during the crop growing period.

Kenya[6]

The evaluation was carried out in six agricultural districts – Kiambu, Makueni, Kwale, Laikipia, Vihiga and Migori – which are distributed across six provinces of Kenya: Central, Eastern, Coast, Rift valley, Western and Nyanza respectively. Owing to great variations in altitude within any given district, rainfall patterns vary immensely. This study assessed five main crops within each district, including banana, beans, maize, potatoes, cowpeas, pigeon peas, sweet potatoes, groundnuts, sorghum, sugar cane, millet and wheat.

The findings suggest that perennial crops (banana, mango, sugar cane) have much higher amounts of evapotranspiration, and hence they are more sensitive to lower water supply than the field crops. However, in all simulations climate change scenarios resulted in high water stress, and lower yields. Having the crop sensitivity information combined with the local water availability and variability provides a powerful policy consideration. For a given crop type, crop water requirements are location specific owing to the marked variability in the agro-ecological characteristics of the study district. However, in spite of seemingly plentiful rainfall, reliable water supply remains the exception in most districts. Certain areas of Kenya are still well supplied with water. Such water assets call for integrated water management at a national level in order to overcome shortages in certain areas, and to support agricultural uses, especially in view of climate change threats.

Niger[7]

Two districts, Aguié and Gaya, and three crops (millet, sorghum and cowpea) were selected for the simulations. The study results show a significant difference for Aguié between the scenarios with and without climate change in 2025 in terms of soil water availability and soil moisture deficit, but this difference is not significant for Gaya, where the decrease in rainfall will maintain adequate soil moisture to support production of subsistence crops such as those included in the simulation.

The findings have important implications for Niger's agricultural policy and the country's strategies for adapting to climate variability and change. Cropping systems may need to change as irrigation will be required for crops that are not adapted to Sahelian conditions. Small farmers could do better if transformed into big units (cooperatives) to increase the irrigation efficiency.

Senegal[8]

The study focused on millet and groundnuts (the main crops in Senegal), and also on maize, which is being developed with the policy of diversification introduced a few years ago. The districts for this study were chosen to represent the spatial rainfall variations. Diourbel and Kaolack are located in the centre of the agricultural basin, in the south Kolda represents the sub-Guinean area. Irrigation and flooded crops are found along the river valleys of northern Senegal, on the northern coast (Niayes) and in the southern part of the country (Casamance).

The simulation results confirm that the districts located in the southern half of the country have a better potential for crop growth. However, it is in this area that an increase in temperature has a negative impact on millet, causing a reduction in yield. Such results call for increased support to agricultural systems in that potentially productive southern region. Adapted crops and varieties should be promoted to counter the negative effects of increased temperatures, in order to sustain rural livelihoods and food security.

South Africa[9]

Crop water use for agricultural production was simulated for major crops, including maize, for 34 districts of South Africa. The results indicate that some areas where large-scale irrigation is practised are in what can be termed arid or semi-arid areas, such as those found along the Orange and Vaal rivers. Detailed analysis of crop water use in the three districts of focus (Lichtenburg, Kroonstad and Middelburg), which represent a spread from the drier western production areas (Lichtenburg) to the wetter eastern areas, is presented here. Most crops in these three districts are rainfed crops (wheat, sunflower, sorghum, legumes and groundnuts) and very little irrigated. The most important crop cultivated in all three districts is maize.

Future crop water use in these areas will be affected not only by climate change within the area but also by the effect a change in climate has on runoff in the catchment areas of the river and thus on irrigation water availability. Climate change that involved a decrease in rainfall would have a large impact on the agriculture of these districts as the most important crops here are rainfed. There is very little potential for increasing irrigation in these districts since there is very little or nonexistent infrastructure for this purpose. However, the impact of climate change on the crop water use to obtain the same level of production as current may not be so high as expected, as the shortening of the production cycle leads to a decrease in water use over time. The reduction in the growth development time of maize may, however, make it more vulnerable to environmental stress such as short drought periods or abnormal weather during pollination. A shortened lifespan means the plant has to go through its critical reproduction period in a shortened time. A stress factor of around 50 per cent also indicated the vulnerability of maize to stress factors in terms of temperature and adverse rainfall patterns.

Adaptation to climate change where the projected scenarios are less water and higher temperatures means, first, more efficient use of water, and second, a change in farming practices. It is, however, important that adaptation takes place at all levels – farm, community and national – to be effective.

Zambia

Cropping patterns including maize, groundnut and cotton in the Chipata district, and maize, sunflower and groundnut in the Chongwe district were selected for the simulation. In the Chipata site, cumulated optimal crop water requirements remain well below the effective rainfall over the same period. This results in virtually no need to complement water supply by irrigation. In the Chongwe site, a cumulated deficit of 111mm, spreading throughout March and April, and peaking during the first ten days of April, means that at best only 75 per cent of required water for that selected cropping pattern was met on average, resulting in decreased yields.

Chongwe district faced severe water deficit, hence stress, at certain periods of cropping calendars. Such deficit may result in severe yield decrease for crops such as maize. Chongwe district hosts most of Zambia's commercial farming systems, and includes most of its irrigation. Since irrigation is still very limited in Zambia, further water resource and irrigation developments should be implemented in order to overcome water stress and risks. The Chipata district is relatively well endowed in rainfall as compared to the needs of typical cropping sequences and patterns. However, observations show that land degradation is a widespread issue, owing to floods, extreme rainfall events, resulting in erosion of slope cultivation.

Overall, the pattern of declining maize production in Zambia, especially among smallholder farmers, indicates that maize is not well adapted anymore to bio-climatic and socio-economic conditions. There is a trend towards cultivating the more profitable, drought resistant food crops such as sorghum, cassava, millet and tubers that use less chemical fertilizers.[10]

Cross section analysis of economic impact

The likely impact of climate change was estimated using the cross sectional approach that was detailed in Chapter 3. Data used for the empirical analysis included household data, district-level data, climate data, soil data and runoff data. The results are reported in this section at the country level. Two types of analyses were conducted. First a marginal impact was estimated, using the cross sectional coefficients only. Then an analysis involving predicted climate scenarios provides more comprehensive estimates of impact. Two types of scenarios were considered. First, a uniform change across the country, and second, specific climate scenarios from global circulation models (GCMs). The GCM scenarios predicted different climate changes in each country over time. Three different GCM scenarios by 2100 are presented in the synthesis to explore the consequences of a range of climate changes that climate scientists believe are plausible. Much more information is provided in the Country Working Papers, as referred to in the footnotes.

Marginal impacts calculations and climatic scenarios calculations

Marginal effects on the agricultural sector of temperature and rainfall changes, resulting from climate change, are calculated for each country on the basis of a marginal change from the mean observed values of temperature and rainfall in the sampled districts.

In addition to examining the marginal impact of climate on current farmers, we also examined a naive climate scenario. In this scenario, the current farmers are exposed to far-future climate scenarios. The analyses examine not the effect of a sudden shock but rather the long-run consequences of facing a different climate.

Several types of climate scenarios were examined. We examined three climate scenarios from climate models that capture the range of climate changes suggested by the literature (Houghton et al, 2001). We include a mild wet scenario (parallel climate model (PCM)), a hotter drier scenario (Centre for Climate System Research (CCSR)), and a very hot scenario (Canadian Climate Centre (CCC)). All these scenarios were country and district specific (due to the vast amount of results, these are not presented but can be found in the country reports). We also examined climate scenarios that involved a uniform change in climate (across country districts or countries). For instance, we looked at warming of 2.5°C and 5°C, and 7 and 14 per cent reductions in precipitation. The advantage of these uniform scenarios is that readers can compare how different places will be affected if faced with the same climate change. Note that we are not implying that the uniform scenarios are equally plausible as the GCM scenarios. The uniform scenarios are simply helpful for understanding the impact of climate change.

Burkina Faso[11]

Highlights from the econometric analysis. Several analyses were conducted, with and without adaptation and with a distinction of the agroclimatic zones. Precipitation and runoff are significant in the model with zone distinction. Temperature effects are not very significant in this model. This means that water is the main factor that explains the spatial variation of revenue in Burkina Faso. The effects of the soils are negative, which can be explained by the low fertility level and low water retention capacity of the soils in Burkina Faso. Irrigation has a positive effect on revenue. As a way of adapting to climate change, it is practised during the dry season and provides farmers with some additional income. During the rainy season it helps to alleviate rainfall hazards and ensure stable production.

   Climate impacts analysis. The marginal effect of temperature and rainfall is calculated on the basis of the average values of the sample (26°C and 717mm in the rainy season and 26.6°C and 80mm in the dry season). No significant difference is observed between the average temperatures for rainfed and irrigated crops. However, precipitation figures for rainfed farms are slightly higher than for irrigated ones for any season. This difference suggests that irrigation is practised where it is necessary because of lower rainfall, but its development depends on the hydrological potential of the region. Therefore most of the drier areas that have water resources develop irrigation.

   The marginal effect of precipitation suggests that when average annual precipitation increases by 1mm, agricultural incomes will increase (Table 4.2) by $2.70/ha on average for all the farms in the sample. The increase will be $2.56/ha for rainfed farms. The increase will reach $3.51/ha for farms that have not adopted certain adaptation strategies. This means that the farmers' current practices mitigate the effect of climatic variability.

Table 4.2 *Burkina Faso: Marginal impact of climate on net revenue ($/ha)*

	Without adaptation		Model with adaptation		Model with zone distinction	
	All farms	Rainfed farms	All farms	Rainfed farms	All farms	Rainfed farms
Temperature	−11.50	−12.20	−19.90	−15.62	−27.07	−21.51
Precipitation	3.51	3.43	2.70	2.56	3.86	3.52

On the other hand, when average temperatures increase by 1°C net agricultural incomes will drop by $19.90/ha for the model with adaptation. This fall in income is weaker for the model without adaptation ($11.5/ha). The effects of climate on income are slightly mitigated in strictly rainfed zones. This means that the rainfed farms are less vulnerable to the effects of climatic changes, maybe because they have already adapted to marginal climates by taking enough precautions to protect their incomes. As the model is based on responses from farmers, it can be said that the rainfed farms have already adopted other strategies of adaptation to the climate change.

The results of the uniform impact analysis are shown in Table 4.3. The increase in the temperature and the reduction in precipitation result in a reduction in incomes with regard to the marginal effects obtained. What is interesting here is to see the extent to which these variations influence incomes. A rise in temperature of 5°C will on average reduce incomes by $135/ha for all farms and $108/ha for rainfed farms. A fall in the annual average precipitation of 7 per cent will mean a total loss of income for all the farms of $215/ha and a lesser loss for rainfed farms of $148/ha. Precipitation impact is more significant and rainfed farms are slightly less impacted in terms of absolute damage.

Table 4.3 *Burkina Faso: Impacts from uniform climate scenarios on net crop revenue*

Scenarios	All farms		Rainfed farms	
	ΔNet revenue ($/ha)	ΔNet revenue (%)	ΔNet revenue ($/ha)	ΔNet revenue (%)
Temperature warming (2.5°C)	−68	−46	−54	−40
Temperature warming (5°C)	−135	−93	−108	−80
Precipitation decreasing (7%)	−215	−148	−196	−146
Precipitation decreasing (14%)	−431	−296	−392	−293

Cameroon[12]

Highlights from the econometric analysis. Net revenues fall as precipitation decreases or temperatures increase across all the surveyed farms. Results of the estimation of Cameroon's estimated net farm revenue response function show that spring and summer temperatures are moderately significant. Winter and spring precipitations are strongly significant. Surface water runoff appears to have a strongly significant influence on farm returns. Results for the socio-economic variables (e.g. farmers' age, education, access to subsidies and extension services, adaptation, etc.) provide important information on the influence of farm values in Cameroon. Cameroon's farmers adapt the agricultural systems and practices to changing economic and physical conditions, by adopting new technologies and changing crop mixes and cultivated acreage (captured in an adaptation specification). Irrigation has a positive impact on net revenue. Few farmers in the country can afford the costs of modern irrigation systems. However, a plethora of rainwater harvesting strategies is employed to cushion the negative impacts of short rainy seasons and long dry seasons in some parts of the country.

Climate impact analysis. Some simple climate scenarios were examined in order to assess how Cameroon's agriculture would be affected by climate change. The marginal impacts were calculated based on mean temperature and precipitation (23.5°C and 283mm/month) across the sampled districts (Table 4.4).

The empirical analysis suggests that a 2.5°C increase in temperatures would cause net revenues from farming in Cameroon to fall by $0.5 billion. Also examined was a 5°C increase that would cause net revenues to fall by $19.5/ha and a 7 per cent decrease in precipitation that would cause net revenues from crops to fall by $26.8/ha (Table 4.5). A 14 per cent reduction in rainfall would cause

Table 4.4 *Cameroon: Marginal impacts of climate net revenue ($/ha)*

Variable	All farms
Temperature	−15.40
Precipitation	5.65

Table 4.5 *Cameroon: Impacts from uniform climate scenarios*

Impacts	2.5°C increased warming	5°C increased warming	7% decreased precipitation	14% decreased precipitation
ΔNet revenue ($/ha)	−7.3	−19.5	−26.8	−45.3
ΔNet revenue (%)	−5.5	−11.3	−20.9	−34.5

significant losses to Cameroon's economy. The significantly negative impacts of rainfall reduction compared to the reduction resulting from temperature increase results from Cameroon's dependence on rainfed agriculture.

Egypt[13]

Highlights from the econometric analysis. Farm size, household size, distance to nearest market, amount of crops sold and quantity of light machinery positively affected net revenue, whereas total cost for labour per farm and amount of crop consumed by livestock negatively affected it. Runoff was found to be positively and significantly correlated with net revenue, which proves that irrigation plays an important role in overcoming heat stress. Farms with big livestock are more sensitive than crop farms.

   Climate impacts analysis. The critical value for marginal impacts is the annual temperature because the seasons' signs offset each other throughout the year; so, we do not examine the sign for each season's weather to see whether it is positive or negative, but rather examine the sign for annual temperature: if it is positive, net revenue will increase; if negative, net revenue will decrease. Results in Table 4.6 suggest that an increase in temperature of 1°C causes a reduction in income of $78/ha without livestock and of $1837/ha when livestock is included. Less favourable results are obtained if runoff, irrigation and heavy machinery are not included in the analysis. The option of raising livestock on the farm as an adaptation for coping with the harmful effect of increased temperature was not effective. In fact, it increased the losses in farm net revenue. This might be attributed to the fact that many of the farmers in the survey were smallholders, who could not afford to use part of their small area to raise livestock.

   Two climate change uniform scenarios were used in the analysis. With runoff, irrigation and heavy machinery, the reductions in net revenue were $116 and $280 per hectare for 1.5°C and 3.6°C increases respectively (without livestock), showing that expenditure on farm machinery could reduce the

Table 4.6 *Egypt: Marginal impact of temperature on net revenue/ha (Model 4*)*

	ΔNet revenue ($/ha)	ΔNet revenue ($/ha) (with livestock included)
Winter temperature +1°C	4109.17	3902.98
Spring temperature +1°C	−107.32	−896.67
Summer temperature +1°C	−7068.05	−6547.89
Fall temperature +1°C	2988.43	1704.41
Annual temperature +1°C	−77.78	−1837.17

* With runoff, irrigation and heavy machinery.

Table 4.7 *Egypt: Impact of climate change scenarios on farm net revenue ($/ha)*

Net revenue	With livestock	Without livestock
Increase of 1.0°C	−1837.20	−77.78
Increase of 1.5°C	−2755.80	−116.67
Increase of 3.6°C	−6613.80	−280.01

harmful effect of temperature increase. Regarding raising livestock on the farms, the results in Table 4.7 show that large losses in farm net revenue would occur using this management practice.

Ethiopia[14]

Highlights from the econometric analysis. Most of the climatic, household characteristics and soil variables have a significant impact on the net revenue per hectare. Both spring and summer temperatures have negative impacts and winter and autumn temperatures have a positive impact. In comparison, the seasons have the opposite impact for precipitation. Winter and autumn precipitation has a negative impact, whereas spring and summer precipitation has a positive effect. The education level of the head of the household and the livestock ownership are positively related to the net revenue per hectare. The distance to input market place is negative, as farmers incur more cost in terms of money and time as the market place becomes further from their farm plots. The household size is negatively related to the net revenue per hectare because there are many dependent and unproductive people in rural Ethiopia (such as children, and the elderly and sick).

    Climate impacts analysis. Increasing temperature during winter and summer seasons significantly reduces the net revenue per hectare. Increasing temperature marginally during the winter and summer seasons reduces the net revenue per hectare by $997.70 and $177.60 respectively. Increasing temperature marginally during the spring and autumn seasons increases the net revenue per hectare by $337.80 and $1879.70 respectively. During spring, a slightly higher temperature with the available level of precipitation enhances germination, as this is the planting season. During autumn, a higher temperature is beneficial for harvesting. It is important that crops have finished their growth processes by autumn, and a higher temperature quickly dries up the crops and facilitates harvesting. Adding the seasonal effects together suggests that warming would increase net revenues per hectare by over $1000. Ethiopia may benefit from warming because the high elevation of many farms implies they currently have cool temperatures.

Table 4.8 *Ethiopia: Marginal impacts of climate on net revenue/ha ($)*

Seasons	Winter	Spring	Summer	Autumn
Temperature	−997.66	337.84	−177.62	1879.69
Precipitation	−464.71	225.09	−18.88	−64.21

Increasing precipitation during the spring season increases net revenue per hectare by $225.10. With slightly higher temperature and available precipitation (soil moisture level), crop germination is enhanced. Increasing precipitation levels during the winter significantly reduces the net revenue per hectare by $464.70. Winter is a dry season, so increasing precipitation slightly with the already dry season may encourage diseases and insect pests. Marginally increasing precipitation during the summer and autumn also reduces net revenue per hectare, by $18.90 and $64.20 respectively, even though the level of reduction is not significant. The reduction in net revenue per hectare during the summer is due to the already high level of rainfall in the country during this season, as increasing precipitation any further results in flooding and damage to field crops. The reduction in net revenue per hectare with increasing precipitation during the autumn is due to the crops' reduced water requirement during the harvesting season. More precipitation damages crops and may reinitiate growth during this season (Table 4.8). Adding the seasonal effects together suggests that a marginal increase in precipitation would reduce net revenues by $323. The more than adequate average level of rainfall in the country indicates that additional rainfall would actually be harmful.

The results of the uniform climate change scenario analysis are shown in Table 4.9. As can be observed from this table, increasing temperature by 2.5°C and 5°C affects net revenue per hectare marginally. Moreover, reducing precipitation by 7 per cent and 14 per cent also reduces net revenue per hectare, even though the level of damage is very small.

Table 4.9 *Ethiopia: Average net revenue/ha impacts of uniform climate scenarios ($)*

Impacts	2.5°C warming	5°C warming	7% decreased precipitation	14% decreased precipitation
Change in net revenue per hectare ($)	−32.0	−43.0	−11.4	−20.7

Kenya[15]

Highlights from the econometric analysis. High summer temperatures are harmful to crop production while high winter temperatures are beneficial. High summer temperatures would therefore slow down or destroy crop growth, while higher winter temperatures are crucial for ripening and harvesting. In the Kenyan highlands winters can be quite chilly, and excessively low winter temperatures have been associated with crop damage from frost. Both autumn and summer precipitations exhibit a hill-shaped relationship with net revenue. The results are robust in that climate exhibits a non-linear relationship with net revenue. The results also imply a hill-shaped relationship between mean flow and net revenue. The results indicate that andosols have a positive and significant impact on net crop revenue, because andosols are quite fertile and thus suited for crop production. Most of the household-level variables (such as education, experience, full-time farming) have a significant impact on crop revenue. Livestock ownership and farm size are inversely correlated with crop revenue. Livestock ownership has a negative impact on net revenue, implying competition rather than complementarity between farming and livestock husbandry. Irrigation has a large positive impact on crop revenue, implying the importance of adaptations to counter the impact of climate change.

   Climate impacts analysis. The marginal impacts for winter temperatures are positive, but summer temperatures have larger negative impacts on net crop revenue. High temperatures are harmful for productivity, confirming that global warming is likely to have devastating effects on agriculture unless farmers take adaptation measures to counter the impact of climate. The marginal impacts of precipitation are more modest than for temperatures; crop revenue is highly sensitive to changes in precipitation, and that increased precipitation increases productivity. A 1 per cent increase in overall rainfall would lead to a $13.34/ha increase in net crop revenue, though a similar change in overall temperature would lead to only a $1.35/ha fall in revenue (Table 4.10).

   The expected impact of a uniform climate change on net crop revenue is shown in Table 4.11. Because of the variation in production regions across

Table 4.10 *Kenya: Marginal impacts of climate on net crop revenue ($/ha)*

Marginal impacts	$/ha
Summer temperature	−59.35
Winter temperature	58.35
Overall temperature	−1.35
Autumn rainfall	8.75
Summer rainfall	4.59
Overall rainfall (1%)	13.34

Table 4.11 *Kenya: Predicted impacts of different climate scenarios by zone[a] ($/ha)*

Climate change scenario	Medium & low potential zone	High potential zone	All zones
+3.5°C	80.05 (24)[b]	−3.54 (−1)	68.45 (20)
+4.0°C	108.79 (32)	11.91 (3)	93.04 (27)
20% reduction in rainfall	69.54 (21)	20.14 (6)	24.39 (7)
+3.5°C + 20% reduction in rainfall	149.59 (44)	16.60 (5)	92.84 (27)
+4°C + 20% reduction in rainfall	178.33 (53)	32.05 (9)	117.43 (34)

Note: (a) The definition of zones is based on Kabubo-Mariara and Karanja (2006, pp8–10).
(b) Percentage change from the sample mean.
Values in parentheses are percentages.

Kenya, the results further suggest that medium and low potential zones are likely to suffer more from rising temperatures resulting from global warming than from a fall in precipitation. However, the reverse is the case for high potential zones and this may be because such zones are located in the highlands where temperatures are quite low and so a rise in temperature may have a lower impact than a fall in precipitation. The whole country is also expected to suffer more from decreases in rainfall than from rising temperatures, just as in medium and low potential zones.

Senegal[16]

Highlights from the econometric analysis. Results of the estimation of Senegal's net farm revenue response function indeed captures the Senegalese reality, with two main seasons: dry and rainy. In the rainy season, an increase in precipitation increases net revenue and an increase in temperature decreases it. The soil variables that were included in the model were generally significant in explaining the variability of net revenues. The size of the household and the presence of male workers have a positive effect on net revenue. The livestock has a positive impact on net revenue. This implies that farmers should keep livestock so as to reduce the variability of crop production, which is strongly dependent on climate variations. The results also confirm the quadratic relationship between net farm revenues and climate variables. Temperature and precipitation have a quadratic relationship with farm net revenues. In addition, annual temperatures as well as seasonal and annual precipitation variables show a positive relationship with farm net revenues, implying that after reaching a minimal point, increases in each of these climate variables yield positive benefits to farm net revenues. There is no significant linear relationship between runoff and net revenue. However, the irrigation variable has a positive sign in this model.

Climate impacts analysis. The analysis of marginal effects of changes in climate attributes indicates that annual high temperature affects farm net revenues positively

Table 4.12 *Senegal: Marginal effect of annual temperature and precipitation change on net revenue ($/ha)*

Variable	Change in net revenue ($/ha)
Annual temperature	−1.17 (−1.6)*
Rainy season temperature	3.55 (2.5)
Dry season temperature	−4.27 (−3.0)
Annual precipitation	6.33 (4.4)
Rainy season precipitation	−1.90 (−1.3)
Dry season precipitation	8.60 (6.0)

Note: * Percentage change from the sample mean.
Values in parentheses are percentages.

(Table 4.12). On the other hand, a 1mm increase in precipitation gives an increase of $16 in net revenue. The results also indicate that seasonal temperature and precipitation also affect farm net revenues. High temperature during the rainy season reduces net revenue whereas precipitation is positive. The implication of these results is that further increases in temperature in the rainy season are detrimental to agricultural activities, as indicated by the negative marginal. During the dry season, an increase in precipitation is beneficial to crop production.

South Africa[17]

Highlights from the econometric analysis. Both 'without adaptation' and 'with adaptation' models were estimated. Climate variables of temperature and precipitation are very relevant for agricultural activities in South Africa and more so for rainfed farming, especially with respect to precipitation. Irrigated farms are cushioned against adverse climate effects by having a substitute for rainwater. The key implications of the 'without adaptation' models are that the extent and nature of the impact of climate factors on crop net revenues may be influenced by the type of soil and the runoff in a particular farming location. Runoff will increase net revenues and also reduce the negative effects of climate but only to a certain extent, as excessive runoff may be detrimental to net revenues. In addition to irrigation and farm type, other socio-economic variables were included. The size of cropland area was found to be important, especially for rainfed farmers, since a larger area enables them to spread their risk from adverse climate effects. Ownership of livestock was also found to be a possible adaptation option, but its effects are different for irrigated and large-scale farms on the one hand and rainfed and small-scale farms on the other. Small-scale farmers and rainfed farmers, especially the latter, are more likely to switch to livestock farming in response to adverse climate effects. Easy accessibility of markets means relatively higher prices for products and therefore helps to cover additional costs caused by the adverse effects of climate.

Climate impacts analysis. Estimated marginal impacts of the climate variables showed that an annual increase of 1°C in temperature will have a positive impact on annual crop net revenues for all farms except rainfed ones. A net increase of $80/ha is expected for the whole of South Africa (increases of $191 for irrigated farms, $588 for large-scale farms and $60 for small-scale farms, but a fall of $50 for rainfed farms). However, what these annual estimates obscure is the seasonal differences in the impacts. Such an increase in temperature will affect crop farm net revenues negatively in the summer farming season but positively in the winter season. The estimates show that including adaptation related variables in the estimation helps increase the positive impacts while reducing the negative impacts for all the types of farming, though not significantly for rainfed farms (Tables 4.13a and 4.13b). Marginal impacts of increase in precipitation exhibit similar signs as in the case of marginal temperature impact. However the level of marginal precipitation impact, both negative and positive, is significantly smaller than that of temperature (Table 4.13b).

Table 4.13a *South Africa: Marginal effects of temperature increase on crop net revenue ($/ha)*

Without adaptation: Climate, soil and hydrology variables model

	Full sample	Irrigated	Rainfed	Large-scale	Small-scale
Summer temperature	952.68	2695.66	−507.20	1892.91	1570.30
Autumn temperature	−1704.20	−5182.81	−605.65	−3279.30	−2595.20
Winter temperature	1561.95	4420.82	997.20	3052.00	2496.52
Spring temperature	−730.56	−1742.35	65.63	−1077.30	−1411.20
Summer–autumn farming season	−751.53	−2487.15	−1112.85	−1386.40	−1024.85
Winter–spring farming season	831.39	2678.47	1062.83	1974.73	
Annual temperature	79.86	191.31	−50.02	588.34	60.48

With adaptation: Climate, soil, hydrology and socio-economic variables model

	Full sample	Irrigated	Rainfed	Large-scale	Small-scale
Summer temperature	918.38	2671.30	−682.28	1302.10	1589.10
Autumn temperature	−1528.60	−5308.30	−197.88	−2177.60	−2376.10
Winter temperature	1516.99	4676.70	687.02	2252.70	2317.18
Spring temperature	−782.62	−1780.70	125.17	−945.37	−1476.90
Summer–autumn farming season	−610.21	−2637.00	−880.15	−875.42	−786.94
Winter–spring farming season	734.37	2896.00	812.19	1307.28	840.32
Annual temperature	124.16	259.04	−67.96	431.86	53.38

Table 4.13b *South Africa: Marginal effects of precipitation (1mm/month increase) on crop net revenue ($/ha)*

Without adaptation: Climate, soil and hydrology variables model

	Full sample	Irrigated	Rainfed	Large-scale	Small-scale
Summer precipitation	30.34	210.66	76.88	−111.31	273.99
Autumn precipitation	−86.09	−447.12	−54.55	104.41	−112.86
Winter precipitation	70.97	417.79	158.78	−76.34	305.29
Spring precipitation	−13.18	−152.81	−160.97	107.95	−494.34
Summer–autumn farming season	−55.75	−236.47	22.33	−6.89	161.13
Winter–spring farming season	57.79	264.98	−2.19	31.60	−189.05
Annual precipitation	2.04	28.52	20.14	24.71	−27.92

With adaptation: Climate, soil, hydrology and socio-economic variables model

	Full sample	Irrigated	Rainfed	Large-scale	Small-scale
Summer precipitation	16.67	160.29	63.53	−100.33	294.04
Autumn precipitation	−54.69	−409.69	−31.08	97.75	−119.84
Winter precipitation	39.47	362.67	120.43	−108.27	311.84
Spring precipitation	−3.91	−96.61	−142.12	98.93	−517.61
Summer–autumn farming season	−38.02	−249.40	32.46	−2.58	174.19
Winter–spring farming season	35.56	266.07	−21.70	−9.34	−205.77
Annual precipitation	−2.46	16.67	10.77	−11.91	−31.58

Zambia[18]

Highlights from the econometric analysis. We note that the net farm revenue is affected by November–December temperature, January–February temperature, January–February wetness and mean runoff. November and December is an important growing period; if the temperature rises at the beginning of the cropping season, when plants are germinating early, this may have a negative effect on the crop. However, for the conditions in Zambia, if the temperature rises during the growing stage of the plant, in January and February this may have a positive effect on the crop.

Climate impacts analysis. The marginal net revenue loss for a unit increase in the mean wetness index (20 per cent increase in precipitation) for January and February is $334/ha. The marginal revenue for a 1cm increase in runoff from the long-term annual average is $3.39. A marginal increase in mean temperature in November–December is harmful (loss of $322/ha) but a marginal increase in mean temperature in January–February has positive impact ($315/ha), as can be seen in Table 4.14. Adding together the seasonal effects reveals that an annual increase in temperature of 1°C would decrease net revenue by nearly $7/ha (315.70–322.62).

Table 4.14 *Zambia: Change in net revenue from uniform climate change scenarios ($/ha)*

Climate scenario	Change in net revenue ($/ha)	Change (%)
1°C increase in mean temperature in November–December	−322.62	−243
1°C increase in mean temperature in January–February	315.70	+237
1 unit of wetness (20% reduction in mean precipitation) in January–February	−334.67	−252
1 cm increase in mean annual runoff	3.39	+2.5

Zimbabwe[19]

Highlights from the econometric analysis. The soil variables that were included in the model were generally significant in explaining variability, mainly in net revenues across households. Among the socio-economic variables, education and increased access to extension services are associated with improved farming information that is important for agricultural productivity. The results also show that small farms are more productive on a per hectare basis than large ones. Other important factors that have significant effects on net farm revenues include access to capital, a high livestock index and access to irrigation. Livestock, particularly cattle, is an important asset in the farming system and can do well in a dry climate. There are further positive relationships between net farm revenues and runoff as an additional source of water for farms with irrigation and all farms and a negative relationship for rainfed farms.

    Climate impacts analysis. An increase in summer temperature of 1°C would reduce net farm revenues by about $86 per hectare for all farms, about $99 for rainfed farms and $77 for farms with irrigation. Increases in the spring temperature also decrease net farm revenues. However, increases in winter and autumn temperatures are beneficial to crops and increase net farm revenues in winter by about $34 per hectare for all farms, about $45 for rainfed farms and $69 for farms with irrigation. Summing these effects across seasons suggests that a 1°C annual warming would reduce farm net revenues across all farms by an average of $57/ha. However, the effect on rainfed farms would be a reduction of $71/ha and the effect on irrigated farms would be a reduction of only $20/ha.

    An increase in precipitation has positive effects on net farm revenues, particularly for summer and spring. An increase of 1mm in summer precipitation would result in an increase in net farm revenues of about $40, $31 and $25 per hectare for all farms, rainfed farms and farms with irrigation respectively. The overall impact of a 1mm/month increase in annual precipitation would be \$131/ha on average. The net incomes of rainfed farms would increase by \$109/ha and the net incomes of irrigated farms would increase by \$102/ha. Revenues are highly sensitive to changes in climate for both temperature and precipitation. Net farm revenues are highly sensitive to changes in climate for both summer temperature and precipitation (Table 4.15).

A uniform climate change impact analysis (Table 4.16) provided several additional insights. Further changes in adverse climate variables (temperature and rainfall) are detrimental to crop production in the country. Rainfed farming is affected most by further increases in temperature and decreases in rainfall. Increases in temperature tend to be beneficial for farms with irrigation, implying that irrigation is important for sustaining agricultural production and as an adaptation option for smallholder farmers. It plays an important role as an additional source of water for crop production, particularly during the dry season and during mid-season dry spells that can affect agricultural production.

Table 4.15 *Zimbabwe: Marginal effects of seasonal temperature and precipitation on net revenue (\$/ha)*

Season	All farms regression	Rainfed regression	Irrigated regression
Temperature			
Summer	−86.34	−98.63	−76.74
Autumn	39.05	32.39	43.28
Winter	34.08	45.44	69.04
Spring	−44.13	−50.36	−55.24
Precipitation			
Summer	39.54	31.29	25.21
Autumn	30.90	22.23	21.80
Winter	23.07	24.30	20.74
Spring	37.80	31.76	34.33

Table 4.16 *Zimbabwe: Impacts on net farm revenue from uniform climate scenarios*

Climate change scenarios	All farms	Rainfed	Irrigated
	ΔNet revenue (\$/ha)		
+2.5°C increase in temperature	−109.93 (−31)	−117.42 (−17)	96.61 (3)
+5°C increase in temperature	−128.84 (−36)	−145.50 (21)	−16.78 (−1)
7% reduction in rainfall	−99.18 (−27)	−112.35 (−16)	−53.82 (−2)
14% reduction in rainfall	−101.97 (−28)	−148.33 (−22)	−77.63 (−2)

Note: Values in parentheses are percentages.

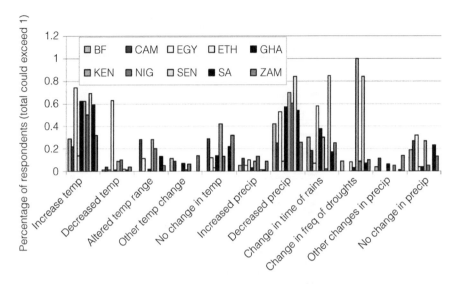

Figure 4.1 Africa: Distribution of perceptions regarding climate change in the ten analysed countries

Note: See plate 19 for a colour version.

Analysis of farmers' perceptions and adaptation strategies[20]

The results of the country-level analysis are very rich and provide interesting highlights on the country-level institutions and culture, and the response of its farmers. Data from Zimbabwe is not included in this analysis because there were problems with the adaptation codes. We start by showing a simple graph (Figure 4.1, plate 19) that presents distribution by country of perceptions regarding climate change. The country acronyms used should be self-explanatory.

An analysis of the perceived barriers to adjustment by farmers in each country provides the other part of the needed explanation to the differences among countries (Figure 4.2, plate 20).

A more detailed description of adaptation and barriers to climate change adjustment is provided in the text below on a country by country basis.

Burkina Faso

The Burkina Faso results are aggregated into three different regions: the Sahelian; the Sudan-Sahelian; and the Sudanese. Over a quarter of those surveyed said that the climate was characterized by increasingly high temperatures. These farmers seem to be concentrated in the Sudanese section of the country. A large

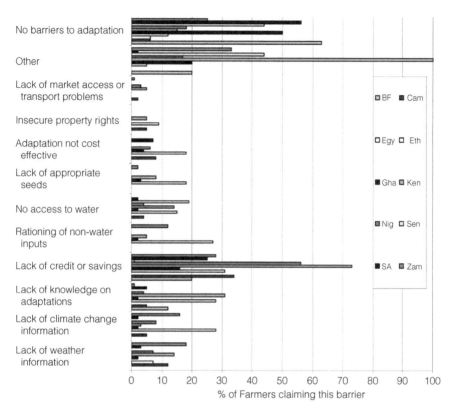

Figure 4.2 Africa: Distribution of perceptions regarding barriers to adaptation to climate change in the ten analysed countries

Note: See plate 20 for a colour version.

number of individuals assert that there has been a change in the pattern of rainfall over recent years. The majority of those questioned appeared to believe that the rains had declined either in terms of quantity of rain or the number of rainy days. These rains are perceived to be less regular and to start and stop unexpectedly. These changes are not uniform across the country and are more pronounced in Sudan-Sahelian areas. In terms of adjustments to these perceived changes in climate, the most frequent responses to higher temperatures and diminished precipitation largely involve changes in organic fertilizer application, techniques to conserve water and retain soil, and reforestation. Changes in kind of crop grown were mentioned by only a small minority of farmers.

Cameroon

The climate's direct impact on sustainable livelihood forces farmers to adopt new practices and coping strategies in response to the altered conditions. Farms and rural households adapt in various ways to lessen the adverse effects of climate variation on crop yield, farm profit and household income. The reported adaptation measures used include:

- shifting crop mix to more drought tolerant and short-season varieties;
- reducing the area planted initially, then increasing it gradually, depending on the nature of the season;
- staggering early or late planting dates;
- increasing plant spacing;
- maximizing the use of clay soils where these are available, since clay soils have a high water-holding capacity;
- implementing soil water conservation techniques (pot-holing, weeding);
- adjusting level and timing of fertilizer;
- undertaking traditional and religious ceremonies.

Crop and soil management techniques include pruning, staking, plant spacing, multiple cropping per year, fallowing, growing solely perennial crops, and zero tillage. In addition to adaptation in general, we specifically identified clusters of farmers who relied predominantly on crop management techniques or soil management strategies as their primary mode for adapting to changing climate, and tested the statistical significance of these options.

Egypt

The results for Egypt present a marked spatial variation in the climate perceptions data. The vast majority of individuals perceive that the climate of Egypt has experienced a change in long-term temperatures. The results for the rainfall impacts are marked in that there are three regions in which almost no one interviewed registered an impact on precipitation. These were the regions of Upper Egypt (Qena, Aswan and Sohag). The explanation is presumably that there is already negligible rainfall in this region. Elsewhere virtually all farmers claimed that they had observed rainfall changes. Recorded adaptations include changes in sowing dates and the use of drought resistant varieties. The number of irrigations per season has increased and they are applied at different times of day. Intercropping is practised with the planting of species with different heights. Mulches are applied and tree planting is undertaken. There is greater use of underground water for irrigation and the use of early maturing varieties.

Ghana

The perception of farmers in Ghana is that the climate has become far hotter. They suggest that there has been a decline in rainfall and a shift in the timing and a reduction in the duration of the rainy season. The soil has become harder to cultivate, seeds have failed to germinate and the leaves of plants have become scorched and wilted. The farmers blame climatic conditions for a reduction in yields. These findings seem to be echoed across all of the regions of Ghana with the possible exception of farmers in the Greater Accra region. Farmers in Ghana report a large number of adaptations to deal with the changes in climate that they have noticed. They have diversified into non-farming activities. They work at different times of day to avoid the heat, and switch to livestock rearing. They use organic manure and weeds as mulch to conserve soil moisture. They engage in multiple cropping and plant new crops better suited to the changed climate. They shade their crops using trees. The timing of fertilizer application is changed and the location of production is changed. Fast-maturing varieties are preferred and some long-maturing varieties have been abandoned. Irrigation is practised in some areas, mainly by hand. Some farmers migrate to the southern part of the country and the more superstitious make increased offerings to deities and ancestors. Obstacles to adaptation include poverty and lack of credit, along with lack of knowledge, market access and problems with transport. Farmers report difficulty in obtaining drugs for their cattle and seeds for more appropriate hybrids of plants such as drought resistant ones. Farmers are reluctant to grow crops that they cannot themselves consume. This suggests that market access in the broadest sense is a problem. Some report problems of insecure property rights. Others suggest that they lack information to know what the appropriate and efficient adaptations are and lack climate information and weather information particularly with regards to the timing of the rains. Many adaptations, however, are simply perceived to be too costly.

Kenya

Nearly half of the farmers in the sample indicated that they noticed a change in climate. Farmers have a range of adaptation measures that they practise, the most popular measure is introduction of different crops and tree planting. Farmers tend to adopt diversification of crop and livestock varieties, including the replacement of plant types, such as drought tolerant varieties. The relatively low proportion adopting adjustments to livestock management could be explained by land scarcity in more arable areas, which may hinder large-scale livestock production. Farmers also use a range of management practices, such as water and soil conservation, to help reduce vulnerability by reducing runoff and erosion, and promote nutrient restocking in soils, while other techniques may improve the soil structure and fertility. Nearly two-thirds of all households that do not adapt are hindered from adaptation due to household poverty. Another fifth fail to adopt any measure because of lack of knowledge concerning appropriate adaptations.

Niger

Adaptations to climate change in Niger include use of mixed and multiple cropping systems. There is a substitution of traditional varieties for early-maturing varieties. There is evidence of substitution between crops towards those that require less water. Sowing dates are changed in order to benefit from changed arrival of the rains. Soil and water conservation techniques are practised more intensively, including the planting of trees. Rituals and prayers are practised in case of drought. Farmers in all regions stress that poverty and lack of information impede adaptation to climate change.

Senegal

The adaptation results in Senegal were grouped into three regions: north, south and the centre of the country. In the north and south of the country farmers detect an increase in temperatures and decrease in rainfall, and a delay in the onset of the rains. Available strategies used by the farmers include a delay in sowing, the use of early-maturing varieties, and techniques to reduce the risks associated with uncertainty of drought. Adaptation includes reduction in area of cultivated land, with some cultivation now taking place on trays. Irrigation is practised in the north of the country. Garden crops are cultivated by women around boreholes. There is a diversification of the activities of the household, and in the centre of the country an exodus to the city.

South Africa

The majority of the interviewed farmers were of the opinion that there had been some change in the climate. This proportion varies across the country. In some areas, such as the Guateng province, all those questioned were of the opinion that the temperature had increased and the amount of rainfall had declined and its timing altered. In the Eastern province, however, less than half of respondents had noticed such changes. Many of the remaining farmers ascribed recent weather patterns to part of a natural cycle. Adaptations to climate change include changes in planting dates and a move towards the use of rapid-maturing varieties. Others resort to the collection of rainwater and increased use of irrigation. Heat tolerant, drought resistant varieties are preferred. Livestock farmers resort to breeds better able to cope with the increased heat. Stocking intensity and location of grazing are altered. Animals are sold at a younger age. Chemicals are used to slow down evaporation. Animal manure is used to maintain soil moisture and more lime is used to balance the soil pH. Many farmers chose irrigation as a means of adaptation and there has been greater use of boreholes and cultivation in naturally marshy areas. Trees are planted for shade. Crop residues are used to maintain moisture and trees planted to prevent erosion. Some large-scale farmers resort to insurance while others have reduced the land under cultivation or have increased involvement in non-farming activities.

Zambia

Some small-scale farmers who felt that the climate had unfavourably altered had switched to other forms of earning income such as trading, charcoal production and brewing. The time of planting has changed and ridge and furrow techniques are adapted to save water.

Zimbabwe

About two-thirds of the farmers observed changes to the climate and indicated that they at least do something in response. The most common adaptation strategies are dry and early planting, which implies access to seed varieties that can stay in the soil for some time before the rains, as well as very early- and short-maturing varieties. In addition there is also a great need for easy accessibility and availability of seasonal climatic forecasts of the oncoming season. Many farmers also use winter ploughing and planting of short-season varieties, use irrigation and grow drought resistant crops. Winter ploughing is very important as it helps conserve moisture especially when it is done soon after the winter rains. But winter ploughing necessitates access to draught power to carry out winter ploughing in time. Because of the reliance on seeds with special characteristics, the insufficient interlinks between farmers and plant breeding companies, research units and the government to ensure the availability of short-season and drought resistant crop varieties may be a barrier to adaptation. A typical example is the case of maize seed that has seen the development of very short-season varieties, such as SC401 and SC403, and medium varieties, like SC501, but have not been introduced widely in the affected regions.

Notes

1. The reader is advised that the analysis using CROPWAT, while simplistic and somehow partial, provides results that are indicative of the set of conditions, both physical and institutional, in each region where it was applied. Compared with many of the comprehensive crop growth models, with more intensive data requirements, the CROPWAT is easier and faster to apply almost anywhere in Africa. This comes of course at the expense of accuracy and comprehensiveness.
2. Based on Some et al (2006).
3. Based on Molua and Lambi (2006a).

4. Based on Eid et al (2006).
5. Based on Giorgis et al (2006).
6. Based on Karanja (2006).
7. Based on Moussa and Amadou (2006).
8. Based in Diop (2006).
9. Based on Durand (2006).
10. In that respect it was brought to our attention by Dr. Peter Cooper that detailed studies on climate change exist in maize growing areas of Zambia that indicate no change in climate, but quite serious decline in soil fertility over the last two decades since structural adjustment and the removal of fertilizer subsidies. This point has been already made earlier, namely that climate change has to be evaluated in the context of other physical and socio-economic and political changes that take place in the continent. Another point for consideration is the wide range of maize varieties with differing growth durations in Zambia, which could be taken into account when designing adaptation strategies.
11. Based on Ouedraogo et al (2006b).
12. Based on Molua and Lambi (2006b).
13. Based on Eid et al (2006).
14. Based on Deressa (2006).
15. Based on Kabubo-Mariara and Karanja (2006).
16. Based on Sene et al (2006).
17. Based on Benhin (2006).
18. Based on Jain (2006).
19. Based on Mano and Nhemachena (2006).
20. Based on Benhin (2006), Deressa (2006), Eid et al (2006), Jain (2006), Kabubo-Mariara and Karanja (2006), Maddison et al (2006), Mano and Nhemachena (2006), Molua and Lambi (2006b), Ouedraogo et al (2006a), Sene et al (2006).

5

Results of the Regional Analyses

While country-level results in the previous chapter are important on their own and could be used for policy making at the country level, or even for comparison between countries in similar agroclimatic zones, an overall regional analysis is important and provides many additional insights. In this chapter we provide the regional-level results from the Crop Water (CROPWAT), hydrology, adaptation and economic impact analyses. The methodologies used in each analysis have been discussed in Chapter 3.

Regional CROPWAT[1]

Farmers in the country sample prefer to grow drought resistant crops (sorghum, pearl millet, groundnuts, etc.) in dry Sahelian areas. Therefore, growing maize in wet areas, or providing timely irrigation can tremendously improve harvest of maize under variable and low rainfall conditions. This trend is also apparent for other crops, although with less observations to make it statistically significant. The water yield curve should, in fact, capture the increased productivity of water. However, since neither crop water use nor actual yield is at its maximum in the selected districts, only the initial slope of that relationship is apparent in the results. The actual crop water use was assessed following the procedures described in Food and Agriculture Organization (FAO) documents (1977). Figure 5.1 displays crop water use in selected districts for the five analysed crops (maize, millet, sorghum, groundnuts and beans).

The results suggest that actual yield of the different crops – specifically of maize and groundnuts – improves with increases in actual crop evapotranspiration, although the gap between the actual and potential yield and actual and maximum evapotranspiration remains high, specifically for rainfed crops. In the case of irrigated crops, the yields are better even when the crop water use is relatively low as compared to their respective water requirement as a result of flexibility in water supply at the critical growth stages of the crops. Rainfed maize and sorghum seem to be performing better in terms of crop water use in the sub-humid climate as compared to semi-arid Sahelian climatic conditions, due to better rainfall. Maize and sorghum appear to be the most water efficient crops grown in the districts.

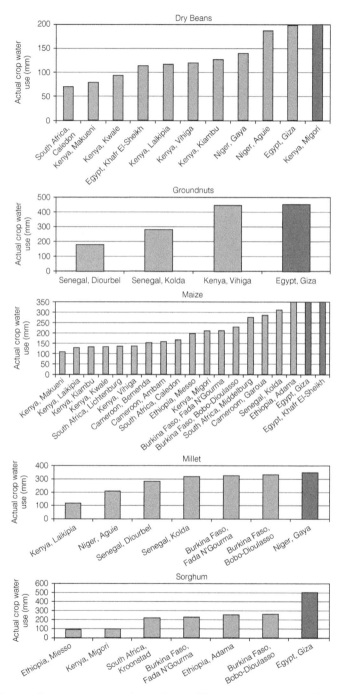

Figure 5.1 Actual crop water use by maize, millet, sorghum, groundnuts and beans in the selected districts in Africa.

Note: Dark grey bars indicate irrigated crop.

Additional analysis of the impact of climate change (increased temperature and CO_2 level) on crop water use and the length of the growing period was applied in selected locations. It is reported here because of its regional importance. Ultimately, CO_2 concentrations are expected to have a positive impact on crop production, and should therefore be incorporated in any impact analysis and its policy consequences. Using the draft Crop Water with Climate Change (CROPWATCC) amended methodology with CO_2 for maize in South Africa, various climate change scenarios were evaluated for their combined impact (temperature and CO_2). The results suggest a significant change in length of growth stages of maize. Depending on the region and the climate change scenario, the reduction in length of growing season for maize varies between 16 and 23 days. There was no reduction in crop yield but crop water consumption was reduced between 1 and 12 per cent in all locations but one.

There are several policy implications that can be drawn from the regional analysis of CROPWAT and CROPWATCC. First, it is clear that there are location-specific conditions that affect the performance of agricultural crops. Second, technological adjustment is a key in adapting to climate in the various locations. It appears from the CROPWAT analyses that irrigation allows farmers to adapt much better, where water is available. The financial/economic aspects have to be further discussed (and this is done in the economic impact analysis, p86), but clearly irrigation provides higher yields that may justify the investment in irrigation. And third, the CO_2 fertilization effect, if correctly incorporated into the analysis, may turn the negative impact of climate change into a positive one by both shortening the growing season and reducing the water requirements of crops. By careful design of the incentive system for both technology adoption and location selection for certain crops, governments could enhance food production and reduce water use even under the severe climatic conditions in Africa.

Hydrology (stream flows)[2]

The hydrology modelling was aimed mainly at estimating the impact of climate change on stream flow across Africa. The data for 1421 political districts in total allowed an Africa-wide analysis with average results for 49 African nations (not only the 11 in the study). The spatial variability of the climate change impacts on stream flows across Africa is presented in Figure 5.2 (see also plate 21). The figures represent the Africa-wide highest and lowest average impact on stream flow for 2050 and 2100.

The policy implications are serious and important to address. They include both the spatial and inter-temporal variability in stream flow, as will be discussed below.

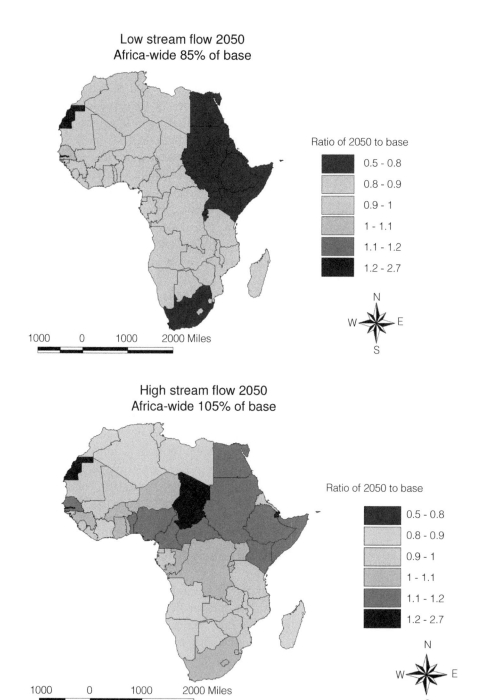

Figure 5.2 Africa: High and low 2050 and 2100 stream flow impacts

Note: See plate 21 for a colour version.

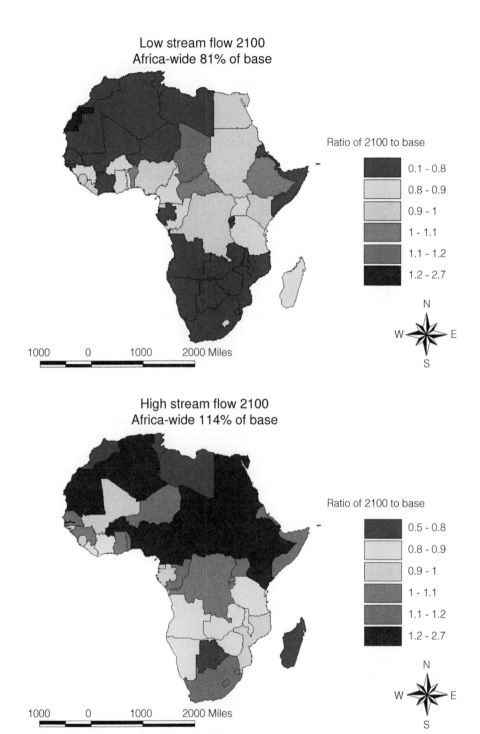

Figure 5.2 *Continued*

General findings

Several important observations from the Africa-wide stream flow impacts in Figure 5.2 include the following findings:

Trends in overall stream flow
- The possible range of Africa-wide climate change impacts on stream flow, by countries, increases significantly between 2050 and 2100.
  - The range in 2050 is from a decrease of 15 per cent to an increase of 5 per cent above the 1961–1990 base.
  - For 2100 the range is from a decrease of 19 per cent to an increase of 14 per cent for a range of 33 per cent.
- The likely continent-wide range of low stream flow in 2050 is reduced from 85 per cent to 81 per cent of the base, and the high stream flow in 2100 is increased from 105 per cent to 114 per cent.
- For southern Africa for all climate change scenarios almost all countries except South Africa experience significant reduction in stream flow.
- For South Africa the increases for 2050 and 2100 under the two high scenarios are modest, at under 10 per cent.

Spatial and inter-temporal variability in stream flow
- Spatial variability across the continent is already big in the base period but it will increase with climate change in 2050 and become even larger in 2100.
- Both the low and the high ranges of inter-temporal flow will widen, introducing both frequent droughts and floods in many African countries.
  - Bracing for these likely events by introducing adaptation measures earlier rather than later should become a priority of the governments and development agencies.
  - Further, coordination among riparian states sharing the same basins should address both water management and dam operations to allow smoothing extreme events when they strike.

Economic impact[3]

The Ricardian crop and livestock models, discussed in Chapter 3, measure the climate sensitivity of net revenues per hectare or per farm, respectively. The models revealed that the net revenues of current African farms are sensitive to climate. Higher annual temperatures tended to reduce crop net revenue but increase livestock net revenue. Higher (lower) annual precipitation tended to increase (decrease) crop revenue but decrease livestock net revenue. Small livestock farmers provide a buffering capacity against climate change impacts to crops. Large livestock farmers are sensitive to higher temperatures just as crops are. More specific results are presented in subsequent sections.

Tables 5.1 and 5.2 below present the sample means of the normal (long-term averages) temperature and precipitation and the number of farms and average current net income per hectare for each country in the study.

Table 5.1 *Africa: Temperature (°C) and precipitation (mm/month) normals (sample means)*

Country	Temperature (°C)				Precipitation (mm/month)			
	Winter	Spring	Summer	Autumn	Winter	Spring	Summer	Autumn
Burkina Faso	23.6	28.3	28.9	24.5	2.6	15.8	113.8	133.1
Cameroon	19.4	21.4	20.0	18.9	60.3	101.9	185.1	228.6
Egypt	11.7	13.2	24.1	23.4	12.8	7.0	2.3	3.5
Ethiopia	18.6	21.5	19.7	18.1	19.4	49.2	123.7	117.5
Ghana	21.8	24.8	22.6	21.2	30.9	59.7	112.4	111.7
Kenya	18.8	19.7	18.4	19.1	88.4	103.0	84.3	60.0
Niger	26.3	30.8	33.9	29.2	0.8	3.2	64.1	70.6
Senegal	24.5	29.1	31.5	26.7	2.2	1.1	47.9	112.7
South Africa	11.5	15.5	20.7	19.4	1.8	55.0	86.4	68.8
Zambia	16.7	21.7	21.1	19.6	48.3	57.7	108.6	100.7
Zimbabwe	16.6	21.3	22.5	20.6	7.5	15.4	138.8	90.0
Africa-wide	19.8	23.4	24.5	22.2	25.9	39.8	96.1	102.4

Note: Seasonal climates have been adjusted so that they are consistent regardless of hemisphere.

Table 5.2 *Africa: Number of useable observations and net revenue per hectare*

Country	Observations			Net Revenue ($/ha)		
	Rainfed	Irrigated	Total	Rainfed	Irrigated	Total
Burkina Faso	990	41	1031	318	538	328
Cameroon	646	105	751	952	1217	987
Egypt	0	802	802	NA	1660	1660
Ethiopia	874	66	940	188	345	199
Ghana	849	29	878	419	496	422
Kenya	675	79	754	255	365	267
Niger	849	48	897	119	227	125
Senegal	1037	31	1068	237	282	239
South Africa	199	87	286	538	1445	811
Zambia	956	14	970	133	145	134
Zimbabwe	597	90	687	403	643	432
Total observations	7672	1392	9064			
Average per hectare net revenue				319	1261	462

Crops

From the cross sectional (Ricardian) models, it is possible to estimate the marginal impact of temperature and precipitation on the net revenues of current farms. For rainfed farms, net revenues, evaluated at their mean temperature, fall by $27/°C. In contrast, the marginal effect of temperature on irrigated farms, evaluated at their mean temperature, is a positive $35/°C. Warmer temperatures increase the net revenues of irrigated farms because the mean temperature in regions with irrigated farms is relatively cooler and because irrigation buffers net revenues from temperature effects. The marginal precipitation effects for rainfed and irrigated farms are more similar ($3.8/mm/month for irrigated and $2.7/mm/month for rainfed farms). The relatively high response of irrigated farms to precipitation is due to their current dry location (Table 5.3).

Marginal impacts of climate calculated at the sample mean are presented in Table 5.3. The analysis also illustrates impacts when regional effects are taken into account. Uniform climate change impact scenarios for Africa (2.5°C and 5°C temperature increase and 7 and 14 per cent precipitation decrease) are presented in Table 5.4. Values per hectare and the total Africa impact suggest a big loss in rainfed in case of temperature increase. Irrigated agriculture gains from temperature rise are between $1.4 and $3.4 billion and rainfed agriculture losses are between $22.6 and $37.7 billion.

Looking at the climate scenarios for 2100 as predicted by several general circulation models (GCMs), we also tested the impact of non-marginal changes in climate assuming nothing else changes. The results show that net revenues from crops will rise in a mild wet scenario by as much as $90 billion across Africa. In contrast, a hot dry scenario could generate losses of $19–27 billion across Africa and a very hot scenario could lead to losses across African farms of $48 billion by 2100. Despite these aggregate impacts, irrigated farms are predicted to generally benefit in these future scenarios partially because they are climate insensitive and partially because they are located in relatively cool locations. Rainfed farms are likely to be affected the most whether it is a benefit of $72 billion or a loss of $44 billion.

Table 5.3 *Africa: Marginal impacts of climate on net revenue ($/ha)*

Sample	Without regional effects			With regional effects		
	Africa	Irrigated	Rainfed	Africa	Irrigated	Rainfed
Temperature	−28.3	−33.6	−23.0	−28.5	−35.04	−26.7
	(1.3)	(0.5)	(−1.6)	(−1.4)	(0.6)	(−1.9)
Precipitation	2.65	2.08	2.02	3.28	3.82	2.7
	(0.36)	(0.06)	(0.47)	(0.44)	(0.13)	(0.63)

Note: Values in parentheses are percentage changes.

Table 5.4 *Africa-wide impacts from uniform climate scenarios*

Impacts	2.5°C warming	5°C warming	7% decreased precipitation	14% decreased precipitation
Rainfed				
ΔNet revenue	−72.2	−120.4	−14.1	−28.3
($ per ha)	(−16)	(−30)	(−6)	(−11)
ΔTotal net revenue				
(billions $)	−22.6	−37.7	−4.4	−8.9
Irrigated				
ΔNet revenue	110.3	258.8	−15.9	−31.5
($ per ha)	(9)	(23)	(−1.4)	(−2.7)
ΔTotal net revenue				
(billions $)	1.4	3.4	−0.21	−0.41
Total (Africa)				
ΔNet revenue	−49.2	−95.7	−18.3	−37.2
($ per ha)	(−11.3)	(−21.9)	(−4.2)	(−8.5)
ΔTotal net revenue				
(billions $)	−16.0	−31.2	−5.96	−12.1

Note: Values in parenthesis are percentage changes.

Livestock

Livestock is an important source of income and food for self-consumption in Africa, and is used as 'insurance' or a cushion during drought years. In our sample livestock consisted mainly of cattle, sheep, goats, pigs and chickens. Food and products sold from raising livestock were milk, meat, eggs, wool and leather (Table 5.5).

Table 5.5 *Africa: Gross revenue from livestock and livestock product sales ($/farm)*

Country	Small farms		Large farms	
	Livestock	Livestock products	Livestock	Livestock products
Burkina Faso	28	11	183	68
Cameroon	173	95	1786	855
Egypt	143	247	5340	1001
Ethiopia	12	59	49	263
Ghana	30	1	347	34
Kenya	32	179	2280	3664
Niger	27	12	142	127
Senegal	31	36	238	83
South Africa	95	40	14,258	4200
Zambia	10	3	1086	1951

The impact of temperature on livestock net revenues depends on the size of the farm. Net revenues of small livestock farms increase by $111/°C. In contrast, the net revenues of big livestock farms fall with warmer temperatures by $397 per degree (Table 5.6). Because large farms have access to more capital and technology, one might expect that large farms would be less vulnerable to warming. However, the most profitable species for large farms are dairy and especially beef cattle, which do not do well in high temperatures. In contrast, small farmers rely on a greater diversity of animals that are more heat tolerant. It is also important to note that large livestock farms specialize in cattle whereas many of the small livestock operations combine crops and livestock. For these small farmers, some of the positive impact of higher temperatures on livestock net revenue comes from substituting livestock for crops. Another aspect that distinguishes small livestock farms from big livestock farms is the ability of small livestock herds to move easily to better grazing locations while big livestock owners, who rely on more sophisticated infrastructure, are less mobile.

A marginal increase in precipitation reduces net revenue per farm for both small and large farms. Small farms decline about $26/mm of monthly precipitation and large farms decline about $60/mm (Table 5.6). Large farms are more sensitive to precipitation than small farms. It may seem strange that livestock values decline with rainfall, since pasture land would generally become more productive as rainfall increases. However, a great deal of African livestock grazes on natural lands. As precipitation increases, natural lands change from nutritious grasslands to forests. It is also true that livestock diseases increase with rainfall.

The impact of a uniform climate change on large and small livestock farms is presented in Table 5.7. Clearly, temperature increase harms large livestock farms (up to 35 per cent reduction in net farm revenue) and benefits small ones (up to 58 per cent increase in net farm revenue). Changes in precipitation impact small and large farms about the same. Note that the table also breaks down the impact per farm into impact on the value of livestock per farm and net revenue per value of livestock per farm. Negative impacts on large farm revenues come from both a reduction in the value of animals and a reduction in the net revenue per animal. By contrast, positive impacts on small farm revenues result from only an increase in the number of animals (Seo and Mendelsohn, 2006a).

Table 5.6 *Africa: Marginal climate effects on small and large farms*

Types	Current livestock income ($/farm)	Marginal temperature impact ($/farm/°C)	Marginal precipitation impact ($/farm/mm)
Net revenue per farm ($)			
Small	104.60	+111.32	−26.05*
Large	3291.03	−397.09*	−59.98*

Note: *Significant at 0.05 level.

Table 5.7 *Africa: Uniform climate change impacts on large and small livestock farms*

Variable	Impact on net revenue per farm %	Impact on value of stock per farm %	Impact on net revenue/ stock value %
Small farms			
Baseline ($)	623	1391	0.37
Increase temperature 2.5°C	+25%	+23%	−10%
Increase temperature 5.0°C	+58%	+48%	−15%
Reduce precipitation 7%	+7%	+5%	+2%
Increase precipitation 7%	−5%	−4%	−1%
Increase precipitation 14%	−10%	−7%	−3%
Large farms			
Baseline ($)	3142	6596	0.40
Increase temperature 2.5°C	−22%	−14%	−17%
Increase temperature 5.0°C	−35%	−25%	−32%
Reduce precipitation 7%	+5%	+5%	+4%
Increase precipitation 7%	−5%	−5%	−3%
Increase precipitation 14%	−9%	−9%	−7%

Future climate scenarios have dramatically different effects on small and large livestock farms. Net revenues for small livestock farms all increase with warming from 25 to 58 per cent. In total dollars, warming leads to a gain of between $2 billion and $6 billion. The net revenues of large livestock owners, however, tend to fall between $14 billion and $16 billion – except for the very dry scenario, which leads to no net effect. The livestock sector in Africa loses from climate change because most animals are in large farms. Small farmers increase livestock earning with warming but these gains are generally smaller than the losses small farmers have in crops.

Cross sectional adaptation[4]

In addition to measuring the impact of climate change on net revenue, we also examined how farmers change their behaviour. We have several analyses that could shed light on actual adaptation of farmers. In Chapter 4 we presented the country-level analysis of perceptions and adaptation options. Here we present the regional analysis that includes the entire dataset from the 11 participating countries. In addition to the adaptation and perception analyses, we performed a set of analyses to understand the mechanism by which various adaptation measures are chosen by farmers. Several farm choices proved to be climate sensitive, including: which crops to grow; whether to own livestock; which livestock to own; how many animals to own; and whether to use irrigation. Separate analyses of each of these choices were made using the cross sectional data, and are summarized below.[5]

Crop choice

The crop choice analysis was aimed at explaining how farmers choose crops as climate changes. The study finds that crop choice is very climate sensitive. The farmers selected 20 different choices of crops to grow. Sometimes they chose a single crop such as maize or wheat but often they chose combinations of crops to grow together such as millet and groundnuts. For example, farmers select sorghum and maize–millet in the cooler regions of Africa, maize–beans, maize–groundnut and maize in moderately warm regions, and cowpea, cowpea–sorghum and millet–groundnut in hot regions. Further, farmers choose sorghum and millet–groundnut when conditions are dry, cowpea, cowpea–sorghum, maize–millet and maize when medium wet, and maize–beans and maize–groundnut when wet. As temperatures warm, farmers will shift towards more heat tolerant crops. Depending upon whether precipitation increases or decreases, farmers will also shift towards drought tolerant or water intensive crops, respectively.

To demonstrate the quantitative nature of our analysis, Figure 5.3 provides a sample of graphs with crop choice probability as a function of climate variables. While the analysis in Kurukulasuriya and Mendelsohn (2006b) includes annual and seasonal climates for various crops and groups of crops, here we present only choice probabilities for annual climates.

African farmers already adapt crop choice to climate. There is every reason to believe that they will continue to adapt in the future. Future farmers may have even better adaptation alternatives with an expanded set of crop choices specifically targeted at higher temperatures.

The results strongly suggest that adaptation policies to climate change must take into account crop selection. Treating crop choice as exogenous will seriously overestimate the damages from global warming. For example, agronomic studies or empirical studies that use weather as a proxy must be careful not to assume crop choices are exogenous. Farmers will probably change crops in response to a new climate rather than repeatedly grow crops that historically were successful but now fail. As a result, farmers will match future crops to future climates. Further, there is an important role for agronomic research in developing new varieties more suited for higher temperatures. Future farmers may have even better adaptation alternatives with an expanded set of crop choices specifically targeted at higher temperatures. Although this may still entail losses in agricultural income in Africa, the predicted losses will be much smaller than if farmers are limited to their current set of choices.

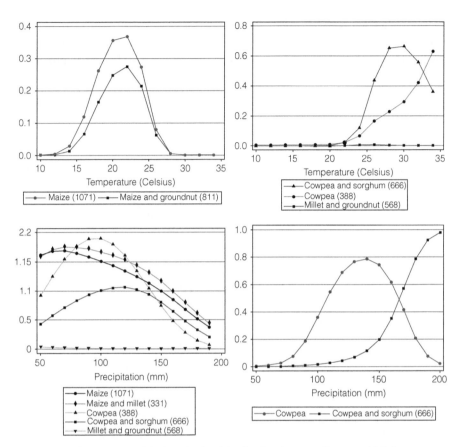

Figure 5.3 Africa: Log odds (vertical axis) of selecting medium and high temperature (first row) and low-medium and high precipitation tolerant crops

Livestock choice

The livestock choice analysis identified five major animals chosen by African farmers, namely beef cattle, dairy cattle, sheep, goats and chickens.[6] Although farmers often have more than one animal, the bulk of net revenue depended on a primary animal in each farm. That is, farmers tend to specialize in a single animal. Large farms are likely to choose beef cattle and dairy cattle, provided temperatures are cool enough. Small farms are likely to select a portfolio of dairy cattle and chickens in most places, and sheep and goats in hotter locations. The livestock choice analysis suggests that beef cattle would become relatively scarce in Africa if temperatures increased but that sheep and goats would become more common.

A question that one should ask is whether farmers even consider owning livestock or only growing crops. This is probably the first choice farmers made before deciding on the size and the mix of their livestock farm. The results in Figure 5.4 indicate that farmers are more likely to own livestock as temperatures rise, and, in all practical circumstances, to get out of livestock growing as

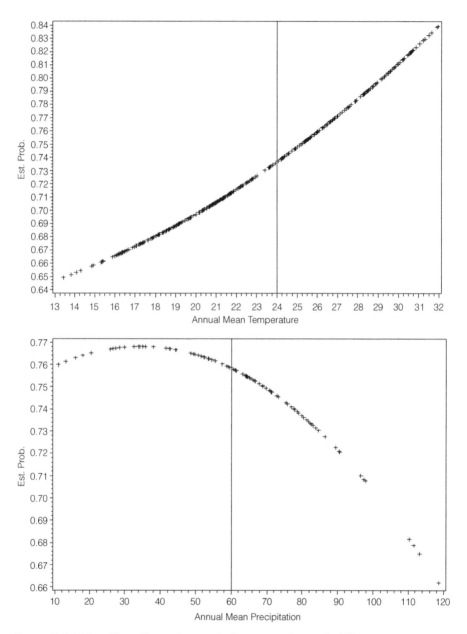

Figure 5.4 Africa: The effect of annual climate on the probability to own livestock

precipitation increases. This getting in and out of livestock is done as a trade-off with crop growing, as resources move between these major activities.

We further estimated the impact of climate on the likelihood of changing livestock mix. As shown in Figure 5.5, annual temperature and precipitation strongly impact the likelihood of choosing different species. With higher temperatures, the likelihood of owning cattle and chickens is reduced and that of owning goats and sheep is increased. With more rainfall, the probability to choose beef cattle, dairy cattle and sheep declines while that of goats and chickens increase.

Farmers in Africa will adapt to warming by slowly moving towards livestock management. Managing livestock in Africa is likely to be relatively more profitable than crops in future climate conditions. However, the mix of species chosen will be slightly different than today, with less emphasis on cattle and chickens and more on goats and sheep. These changes may be especially hard on larger farms that currently specialize in cattle. Although we anticipate that there will be widespread adaptations for small farmers, farmers should be able to make these transitions if climate change gradually unfolds and they are suitably advised by husbandry experts in extension services.

Number of animals

We also estimate how the number of each animal owned by farm changes across Africa. In this analysis, farmers were assumed to face several simultaneous decisions. Once a species has been defined as producing the greatest net revenue it is selected as the primary animal, then the farmer decides on the number of animals of that type per farm.

Farmers will adopt more animals of a given species as they become more profitable. In Africa, the ideal climate conditions for livestock, especially cattle, are warm and dry (grasslands but not desert) climates. With increased precipitation, the landscape turns to forest, which reduces forage for grazing animals. Higher temperatures turn the warm grasslands into desert. Consequently, both higher temperatures and more precipitation decrease the number of animals that farmers choose to own, especially beef cattle. But some animals such as dairy cattle, sheep and goats are raised widely across Africa. These animals will likely survive future climate change and become the resorts of African farmers in responding to climate change. An example of the change in probability of selecting sheep as temperature rises in Africa is presented in Figure 5.6 (plate 22).

The analysis suggests that farmers just south of the Sahara will switch species, diversify their portfolio of animals, and move away from cattle and towards sheep. Small farmers will be able to make these changes without much change in expected net income. In contrast, large sheep farmers in South Africa will have to abandon sheep. These changes are predicted to reduce the net

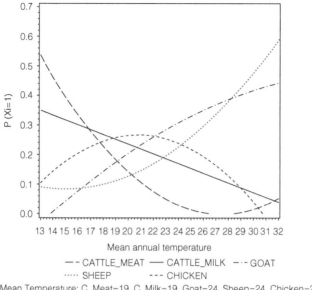

Mean Temperature: C_Meat=19, C_Milk=19, Goat=24, Sheep=24, Chicken=21

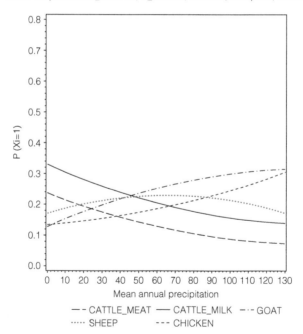

Mean Precipitation: C_Meat=58, C_Milk=63, Goat=68, Sheep=59, Chicken=76

Figure 5.5 Africa: The effect of annual climate on the probability of livestock species choice (primary animal approach)

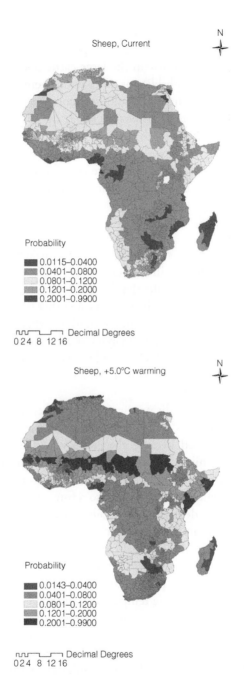

Figure 5.6 Africa: Change in probability of choosing sheep in Africa with a uniform temperature increase of 5°C

Note: See Plate 22 for a colour version.
Source: Seo and Mendelsohn, 2006b.

incomes of large farms considerably. African policy makers must be careful to encourage private adaptation during this period of change. There may be nothing that can be done to sustain the large cattle operations that depend on current climate. Providing subsidies or other enticements for such operations to continue once the climate changes would only compound the problem. Instead, governments should encourage farmers to change the composition of animals on their farms as needed. That is, they should inform farmers about how other livestock owners have coped with higher temperatures and share indigenous knowledge. Governments should anticipate that farmers will make changes on their lands and do whatever is needed to facilitate these changes.

Irrigation choice

One of the biggest questions facing African policy makers is the possible role of irrigation in food production in general, and as an adaptation measure in the context of climate change. Results that have been reported in Chapter 4 and in previous sections of this chapter already indicated that irrigated agriculture is less vulnerable than rainfed agriculture, in all locations where water for irrigation is available. However, these previous analyses treated irrigation as an exogenous incident. While doing so provides 'first order estimates' of the role of irrigation, it is more appropriate to recognize that farmers choose irrigation and that this choice is sensitive to climate.

The irrigation analysis indicates that climate affects whether or not a farmer would choose irrigation. As precipitation becomes plentiful, the high cost of irrigation is not warranted because the crops would do almost as well with rainfed techniques. Similarly, high temperatures discourage irrigation because they lower productivity. In Africa, places that are cool are much more likely to adopt irrigation. Of course, irrigation is also a function of water availability.

Figures 5.7 and 5.8 depict the probability of choosing irrigation as affected by seasonal temperature and seasonal precipitation. Because irrigation is used for various crops, we present the seasonal climates rather than the annual ones. As the figures show, increased winter, summer and autumn temperatures and increased winter and summer precipitation reduce the likelihood that irrigation will be selected. Increased spring temperature and increased spring and autumn precipitation increase the likelihood that irrigation is adopted.

Estimation of the marginal impact effects of climate change on irrigated and rainfed agriculture with endogenous irrigation technology selection (adaptation) is presented in Table 5.8. One of the most important results is the difference in mean net revenue between irrigation and rainfed agriculture that amounts to nearly $950/ha per year. This figure could be the basis for calculations of profitability of investments in irrigation in Africa, just to account for climate change impacts.

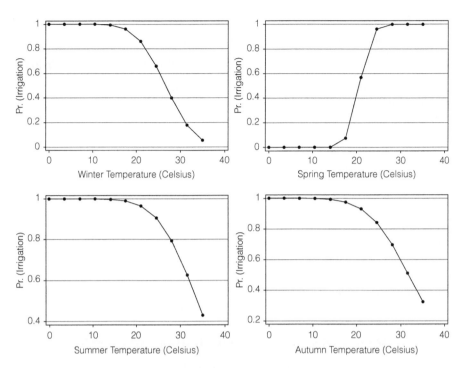

Figure 5.7 Africa: Seasonal temperature and probability of adopting irrigation

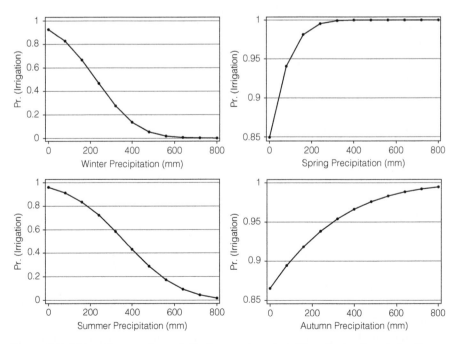

Figure 5.8 Africa: Seasonal precipitation and probability of adopting irrigation

Table 5.8 *Africa: Marginal annual climate (temperature and precipitation) impacts on net revenue of rainfed and irrigated agriculture*

	Rainfed	Irrigated
Mean net revenue ($/ha)	325.7	1283.8
Mean annual temperature (°C)	23.2	19.6
Mean annual precipitation (mm/month)	34.4	71.6
Marginal temperature effect ($/ha)	−11.34	17.37
Marginal precipitation effect ($/ha)	2.62	−0.22

Note: Values are calculated at the mean of the rainfed and irrigated samples.

Irrigation is an effective adaptation against reduction in rainfall and higher temperatures provided there is sufficient water available. This will be an effective remedy in select regions of Africa with water. However, for many regions, there is no available surface water, so that warming scenarios with reduced rainfall are particularly deleterious.

Perception of climate change, adaptation practices and barriers

The preliminary evidence from the country-level information that was described in Chapter 4 reveals that large numbers of farmers already perceive that the climate has become hotter and that the rains have become less predictable and shorter in duration. Some farmers did not observe changes in climate. For example, 42 and 27 per cent of the farmers in Kenya who did not observe changes in temperature and precipitation, respectively.

The perception of climate change was tackled by three alternative analyses. The first analysis examines whether perceptions of climate change are dependent on experience. One would suspect that more experienced farmers should be able, more easily, to distinguish climate change from what is merely inter-annual variation. The second analysis considers whether the assessments of individual respondents can be validated by the responses of neighbouring farmers. The third analysis considers whether farmers' perceptions of climate change correspond to the evidence of changes provided by nearby climate monitoring stations. If they do not, then farmers reveal themselves in dire need of help.

Table 5.9 provides country-level averages for shares of farmers' responses to the particular perception questions.

The data indicates that across the countries studied significant numbers of individuals believed that average temperatures have increased. The results for precipitation show a similar uniformity of opinions. A sizeable minority also

Table 5.9 *Africa: Shares of farmers' perceptions of climate change by country*

Perception	Burkina Faso	Cameroon	Egypt	Ethiopia	Ghana	Kenya	Niger	Senegal	South Africa	Zambia
Increased temperatures	0.29	0.22	0.74	0.14	0.62	0.62	0.50	0.69	0.59	0.32
Decreased temperatures	0.01	0.04	0.01	0.63	0.01	0.09	0.10	0.02	0.01	0.04
Altered temperature range	0.00	0.28	0.11	0.00	0.02	0.28	0.20	0.00	0.13	0.05
Other temperature change	0.11	0.09	0.00	0.00	0.07	0.01	0.06	0.00	0.00	0.14
No change in temperature	0.00	0.29	0.12	0.03	0.14	0.42	0.13	0.00	0.22	0.32
Increased precipitation	0.05	0.11	0.05	0.10	0.03	0.09	0.13	0.01	0.01	0.09
Decreased precipitation	0.42	0.25	0.53	0.09	0.57	0.70	0.60	0.84	0.54	0.26
Change in timing of rains	0.30	0.18	0.07	0.58	0.38	0.30	0.02	0.85	0.17	0.25
Change in frequency of droughts	0.09	n.a.	0.00	0.08	0.03	1.00	0.09	0.84	0.07	0.10
Other changes in precipitation	0.04	0.11	0.00	0.00	0.06	0.00	0.05	0.00	0.01	0.14
No change in precipitation	0.19	0.27	0.32	0.04	0.04	0.27	0.05	0.00	0.23	0.13

believed that they had witnessed a change in the timing of the rains. Very few farmers believed that they had lived through a change in the frequency of droughts although there is an exception in the case of Senegal and Kenya where almost everyone believed that they had witnessed a change in the cycle of droughts.

The next question that one can ask is whether farmers' perceptions tally with weather monitoring station records. Temperature and precipitation data was taken from the Africa Rainfall and Temperature Evaluation System (ARTES) dataset (see Chapter 3) and values at village localities were compared to farmers' perceptions on precipitation and temperature trends in a particular village. Burkina Faso, Cameroon, Egypt, Ethiopia, Ghana and Zambia have indeed experienced significantly higher temperatures, whereas Kenya, Ghana, Niger, Senegal and Zambia have experienced a significantly drier climate. A large share of farmers in the samples in those countries are therefore correct in saying that the climate has become hotter and drier. However, there are a number of countries (Kenya, Niger, Senegal and South Africa) where a large share of farmers in the sample state that the climate is becoming hotter despite no evidence for such a change in the meteorological records. Likewise there is no evidence that precipitation has changed over Egypt, Kenya and South Africa although a large share of farmers in the sample claim that the climate has become drier.

What do these results mean from a policy point of view? Do farmers who believe that climate has changed also adapt? What kind of adaptation measures do they apply (Box 5.1)? Are human capital and information services critical? What can governments do to improve farmers' ability to adapt? We look at differences in adaptation rates according to socio-economic characteristics, and perceptions of climate change, taking into account baseline climate accounting for prior adoption. We will also distinguish between individuals who perceived climate change but did not adapt in any way. Such individuals may be experiencing barriers to adaptation, so their characteristics are of particular interest.

In all countries apart from Cameroon and South Africa, the planting of different varieties of the same crop is considered to be one of the most important adaptation measures. Different planting dates are also considered an important adaptation in Egypt, Kenya and Senegal. Adopting a shorter growing season is universally practised in Senegal but is elsewhere almost irrelevant. In Egypt the majority of respondents have moved towards non-farming activities. In Egypt, Kenya and South Africa significant numbers of farmers have adapted by increased use of irrigation. In Burkina Faso, Kenya and Niger there is increasing use of water conservation techniques. Soil conservation techniques are increasingly practised in Burkina Faso, Kenya, Senegal and Niger. There is also increasing use of shading and sheltering techniques in Burkina Faso, Niger and

Box 5.1 List of adaptation measures reported in Africa

Different varieties
Different crops
Crop diversification
Different planting dates
Shortening growing season
Lengthening growing season
Moving to a different site
Changing quantity of land under cultivation
Change from crops to livestock

Change from livestock to crops
Adjustments to livestock management
Change from farming to non-farming activity
Change from non-farming to farming activity
Increased use of irrigation/groundwater/watering
Decreased use of irrigation/groundwater/watering
Changed use of capital and labour
Changed use of chemicals and fertilizers

Increased use of water conservation techniques
Decreased use of water conservation techniques
Soil conservation techniques
Shading and sheltering/tree planting
Use of insurance or weather derivatives
Prayer or ritual offering
Other
No adaptation

Senegal. Increased use of weather insurance is almost exclusive to Egypt. Prayer and ritual offerings are made in Senegal and Niger. There are, however, several countries in which almost a third or more of respondents report no change in agricultural practices. These include Burkina Faso, Cameroon, Ghana, South Africa and Zambia. By contrast every Egyptian and every Ethiopian interviewee claimed to have made one adaptation.

How does baseline climate affect adaptation? Do farmers in already hotter, cooler, drier, wetter, high runoff or low runoff climates behave differently? The results suggest that irrespective of the nature of the baseline climate, changing the varieties grown appeared to be an important adaptation. Shortening the growing season was also very important but only in climates that were currently either hot or dry or had low runoff. Changes to non-farming activities took place in areas that were cool and dry with low runoff and therefore seemingly inappropriate for agriculture. Such changes were not observed where the climate was already hot and wet. Increased use of water and soil conservation techniques was noted in regions that were already hot and dry with low runoff. Shading and sheltering techniques were also noted in those areas that were hot and dry with low runoff.

A binary model (yes/no) was used to assess whether or not the farmer registers a particular perception of climate change, and explained it by a range of variables including farmer experience, age, years of education, gender, marital status, whether he is the head of the household or not, whether he engages in off-farm work, and the country of residence. Distance to market, an indicator for subsistence farming, and whether or not any extension advice given to the farmer included information on climate were used too. These results are adjusted for clustering at the level of the village on the assumption that the responses from farmers in the same village are likely to be related anyway. Experienced farmers are more likely to perceive change in the climate. Distance to market where the farmers buy their inputs or sells their outputs, and exchange information with others, seems to make a critical difference where farmers with more access to market are likely to perceive change in climate. Subsistence farmers are far more likely to notice climate than other sorts of farmers.

Adaptation to climate change involves a two-stage process – first perceiving that climate change has occurred and then deciding whether or not to adopt a particular measure. The results indicate that the adaptation process is driven by a number of factors. Firstly, more experienced farmers are more likely to record an adaptation measure. Being in receipt of extension advice relating either to livestock or crop production also strongly increases the probability of adaptation. The education of the respondent (measured in years) also greatly increases the probability of adaptation. All of these have obvious implications to the question of what can be done to help farmers adapt to climate change. Being head of the household also increases the probability that the farmer can adapt, perhaps because he or she is in control of household resources. There is, however, no evidence that gender influences the probability of adaptation. Individuals farming rented land appear less willing or able to adapt, possibly because they might be relieved of their land. There is strong evidence that current climate influences the probability of adaptation.

There are very marked differences in the ability of farmers from different countries to respond to change in climate. Farmers in Burkina Faso are much less likely to respond whereas farmers in Egypt almost invariably respond. The precise reasons underlying such differences could not be verified from the available data. They may be related to the quality of institutions, the existence of infrastructure, differences in prices or simply a manifestation of the way in which the survey was conducted and the data input.

An important policy question is whether agricultural adaptation in the face of climate can be expected to occur autonomously or whether government has a role in intervening. The results of this study make it clear that at least some adaptation takes place autonomously. For all sample countries, we found that governments could have an important role in promoting certain aspects.

In terms of policy implications it appears that improved farmer education would do most to hasten adaptation. The provision of free extension advice may also play a role in promoting adaptation. In so far as distance to the selling market is a significant determinant of whether a farmer adapts to climate change, it may be that improved transport links would improve adaptation, although the precise mechanism underlying this is unclear. Better roads may allow farmers to switch from subsistence farming to cash crops, or facilitate the exchange of ideas through more regular trips to the market.

There are many country-specific differences in the propensity of individuals to adapt, and further analysis would be required to understand underlying factors. Adaptation, however, is something undertaken only by those who perceive climate change. The perception of climate change appears to hinge on farmer experience and the availability of free extension advice specifically related to climate change. But while the policy options for promoting an increased awareness of climate change are more limited, earlier analysis indicates that the perception of climate change is already high.

Notes

1. Based on Wahaj et al (2006).
2. Based on Strzepek and McCluskey (2006).
3. Based on Kurukulasuriya and Mendelsohn (2006a, 2006b), Seo and Mendelsohn (2006a, b, c).
4. Based on Maddison (2006), Kurukulasuriya and Mendelsohn (2006b) and Seo and Mendelsohn (2006a, 2006b).
5. A simultaneous analysis of all adaptation options will be performed at a later stage.
6. Seo and Mendelsohn (2006b) use three approaches (primary animal approach, demand system approach and portfolio approach), but we report only the primary animal one.

Summary, Conclusions and Policy Implications

In Chapter 1, we had to rely on imported coefficients to assess the impact of climate change on agriculture in Africa. This was in 2000. At that time we did not have any idea of how adaptation in the agricultural sector worked. We reviewed the literature (Annex 1), from which we were able to get some anecdotal information on adaptation. The review of the literature suggested that there are already adaptation measures that farmers are undertaking in different parts of Africa. The literature review suggested that there are also available technologies and management practices that were produced by research institutes, either regional or local ones. However, we could not quantify the value of all these adaptation measures that have been available.

The estimated impact of climate change, using the imported coefficients in Chapter 1, provided the needed urgency for the study. The range of estimated impacts and its distribution among the countries in the African continent was alarming. Therefore, the main goal of the study 'Climate Change Impacts on and Adaptation of Agro-ecological Systems in Africa' was to develop multipliable analytical methods and procedures to assess quantitatively how climate affects current agricultural systems in Africa, predict how these systems may be affected in the future by climate change under various global warming scenarios, and suggest what role adaptation could play. The study countries covered all key agroclimatic zones and farming systems in Africa. This is the first analysis of climate impacts and adaptation in the Africa continent of such scale and the first in the world to combine cross-country, spatially referenced survey and climatic data for this type of analysis.

The analyses in this report focus mainly on quantitative assessment of the economic impacts of climate change on agriculture and the farming communities in Africa, based on both the cross sectional (Ricardian) method and crop response simulation modelling. The cross sectional analysis also allowed for assessing the possible role of adaptation. Moreover, the project employed river-basin hydrology modelling to generate additional climate attributes for the impact assessment and climate scenario analyses such as surface runoff and stream flow for all districts in the study countries.[1]

The results suggest that Africa will be hit hard by severe climate change under various scenarios. Some countries are more vulnerable than others, so it is important to focus on the countries that really need help. In fact, in several scenarios, many African farmers gain whereas others lose from climate change. This study also notes that African farmers already practise some forms of climate adaptation.

The studies focus on the costs privately borne by farmers and livestock holders while adjusting to (perceived) climate variability. These costs were computed in terms of lower Ricardian land rent. Ricardian rents with adaptation are based on observed farmers' behaviour with a large set of existing technologies across a wide range of present climates with no CO_2 fertilization effect. Therefore Ricardian analyses provide a lower value for estimates of future adaptation compared to what it could have been with future technologies and CO_2 enrichment.

In what follows we will introduce conclusions and policy implications from the various levels and types of the analyses. We will start with the analyses at the country level, move to regional analyses, and end up with general (continental) policy implications.

Country-level analysis of climate change impacts on crop water requirements

The application of the Crop Water (CROPWAT) to selected regions in each country allowed the generation of some simulations that provide insight into hotspots and possible adaptation options. These insights should be read keeping in mind the caveats elaborated in Chapters 1 and 4, namely that certain African countries are already experiencing changes that are related to natural resources quality and availability. Such changes may interfere with the impact of climate change. Therefore, carefully accounting for soil degradation, social pressure on natural resources, and existing institutions is essential for proper evaluation of impacts and adaptation effectiveness.

Burkina Faso

The main outcome of the analysis shows that soil's water-holding capacity is low in Burkina Faso. In the southern part of the country, water requirements for cereal crops and groundnut are met from rainfall. In the Sudano-Sahelian and Sahelian regions, water deficits are experienced towards the end of the rainy season. Supplementary irrigation is needed to enable cereal crops to finish their cycle normally. In the cotton belt, irrigation needs for cotton and maize are very low, but in the centre, the north and the Sahel, irrigation needs at the end of the season are substantial.

Cameroon

The findings in Cameroon indicate that even though farmers may be adapting to climatic variation, additional resources and irrigation infrastructure are needed, especially in the drier northern parts of the country, to counter the debilitating effect of low soil moisture, peaking daily temperatures and runaway evapotranspiration. To ease water constraints and enhance productivity, there is a need to cultivate drought tolerant crops and improve irrigation by switching from traditional to more efficient systems such as drip irrigation and pipe irrigation.

Egypt

Climate change could increase crop water use and reduce yields in Egypt. Strategies for adapting to climate change may involve the development of new, more heat tolerant cultivars, and new crops (more cotton cultivation as an alternative to some maize, and more winter legumes instead of some wheat). Changing the cotton crop practices (optimum sowing date, cultivars, water and nitrogen amounts and plant density) could allow farmers to benefit from new varieties or technologies. Further adaptation may modify the cropping pattern (i.e. partly growing cotton after wheat in the same year and on the same land) and reduce current area under some high water use crops (i.e. sugar cane and rice).

Ethiopia

Various adaptive measures can be considered, such as using supplementary irrigation and water harvesting, minimizing evaporative demand by using mulch, and applying soil moisture conservation techniques and crop management practices that reduce sensitivity to water stress. Most of these adaptive measures are undertaken at farm level depending on farmers' perceptions of water stress conditions. In the two districts studied, farmers are also adjusting planting density and the timing of various operations, and using conservation tillage and intercropping.

Kenya

The findings in Kenya suggest that perennial crops (banana, mango, sugar cane) have much higher amounts of evapotranspiration, hence they are more sensitive to lower water supply than field crops. However, in all simulations climate change scenarios resulted in high water stress, and lower yields. For a given crop type, crop water requirements are location specific owing to the marked variability in the agro-ecological characteristics of the study district. Certain areas of Kenya are still well supplied with water. Such assets call for integrated water management at national level in order to overcome shortages in certain areas, and to support agricultural uses, especially in view of climate change threats.

Niger

Cropping systems in Niger may need to change as irrigation will be required for crops that are not adapted to Sahelian conditions. Small farmers could do better if transformed into big units (cooperatives) to increase the irrigation efficiency.

Senegal

The results in Senegal confirm that the districts located in the southern half of the country have a better potential for crop growth. However, it is in this area that an increase in temperature has a negative impact on millet, causing a reduction in yield. Such results call for increased support to agricultural systems in the potentially productive southern region. Adapted crops and varieties should be promoted to counter the negative effects of increased temperatures, in order to sustain rural livelihoods and food security.

South Africa

Adaptation to climate change in South Africa, where the projected scenarios are less water and higher temperatures, means first, more efficient use of water, and second, a change in farming practices. It is, however, important that adaptation takes place at all levels – farm, community and national – to be effective.

Zambia

Overall, the pattern of declining maize production in Zambia, especially among smallholder farmers, indicates that maize is not well adapted anymore to bio-climatic and socio-economic conditions. There is a trend towards cultivating the more profitable, drought resistant food crops such as sorghum, cassava, millet and tubers that use less chemical fertilizers.

Farmers reported adaptation strategies and barriers to adaptation

While our quantitative analyses focus on quantifying adaptation options and their likelihood (irrigation, crops, livestock), we collected data that could be critically useful for policy. Farmers' perceptions about adaptation to climate change[2] and barriers affecting them were collected in the various countries. They are reported below. The overall analysis has quite important policy relevance.

Burkina Faso

In terms of adjustments to these perceived changes in climate, the most frequent responses to higher temperatures and diminished precipitation largely involve changes in organic fertilizer application, techniques to conserve water and retain soil, and reforestation. Changes in kind of crop grown were mentioned by only a small minority of farmers.

Cameroon

The reported adaptation measures used, include several management and spiritual practices such as crop types, planting dates, conservation practises and undertaking traditional and religious ceremonies. Specific management practises include: shifting crop mix to more drought tolerant and short-season varieties; reducing the area planted initially, then increasing it gradually, depending on the nature of the season; staggering early or late planting dates; increasing plant spacing; maximizing the use of clay soils where these are available, since clay soils have a high water-holding capacity; implementing soil water conservation techniques (pot-holing, weeding); and adjusting level and timing of fertilizer.

Crop and soil management techniques include: pruning, staking, plant spacing, multiple cropping per year, fallowing, growing solely perennial crops, and zero tillage.

Egypt

Recorded adaptations include changes in sowing dates and the use of drought resistant varieties. The number of irrigations per season has increased and they are applied at different times of day. Intercropping is practised with the planting of species with different heights. Mulches are applied and tree planting is undertaken. There is greater use of underground water for irrigation and the use of early maturing varieties.

Ghana

Many farmers in Ghana have diversified into non-farming activities, work at different times of day to avoid the heat and switch to livestock rearing. They use organic manure and weeds as mulch to conserve soil moisture, engage in multiple cropping and shade their crops using trees. The timing of fertilizer application and location of production have changed. Fast-maturing varieties are preferred and some long-maturing varieties have been abandoned. Irrigation is practised in some areas. Some farmers migrate to the southern part of the country and the more superstitious make increased offerings to deities and ancestors. Obstacles to adaptation include poverty and lack of credit, along with lack of knowledge, market access and problems with transport. Farmers report difficulty in obtaining drugs for their cattle and seeds for more appropriate hybrids of plants such as drought resistant ones. Farmers are reluctant to grow crops that they cannot themselves consume. This suggests that market access in the broadest sense is a problem. Some report problems of insecure property rights. Others suggest that they lack information to know what the appropriate and efficient adaptations are and lack weather information, particularly with regards to the timing of the rains. Many adaptations, however, are simply perceived to be too costly.

Kenya

Farmers tend to adopt diversification of crop varieties, including the replacement of plant types, such as drought tolerant varieties. The relatively low proportion adopting adjustments to livestock management could be explained by land scarcity in more arable areas, which may hinder large-scale livestock production. Farmers also use a range of management practices, such as water and soil conservation, to help reduce vulnerability by reducing runoff and erosion, and promote nutrient restocking in soils, improving soil structure and fertility. Nearly two-thirds of all households that do not adapt are hindered from adaptation due to household poverty. Another fifth fail to adopt any measure because of lack of knowledge concerning appropriate adaptations.

Niger

Adaptations to climate change in Niger include use of mixed and multiple cropping systems. There is a substitution of traditional varieties for early-maturing varieties. There is evidence of substitution between crops towards those that require less water. Sowing dates are changed in order to benefit from changed arrival of the rains. Soil and water conservation techniques are practised more intensively, including the planting of trees. Rituals and prayers are practised in case of drought. Farmers in all regions stress that poverty and lack of information impede adaptation to climate change.

Senegal

Available strategies used by the farmers include a delay in sowing, the use of early-maturing varieties, and other techniques to reduce the risks associated with uncertainty of drought. Adaptation includes reduction in area of cultivated land, with some cultivation now taking place on trays. Irrigation is practised in the north of the country. Garden crops are cultivated by women around boreholes.

There is a diversification of the activities of the household, and in the centre of the country an exodus to the city.

South Africa

Adaptations to climate change include changes in planting dates and a move towards the use of rapid-maturing varieties. Others resort to rainwater harvesting and increased use of irrigation. Heat tolerant drought-resistant varieties are preferred. Livestock farmers resort to breeds better able to cope with the increased heat. Stocking intensity and location of grazing are altered. Animals are sold at a younger age. Chemicals are used to slow down evaporation. Animal manure and crops' residue are used to maintain soil moisture and more lime is used to balance the soil pH. Many farmers chose irrigation as a means of adaptation and there has been greater use of boreholes and cultivation in naturally marshy areas. Trees are planted for shade and to prevent erosion. Some large-scale farmers resort to insurance while others have reduced the land under cultivation or have increased involvement in non-farming activities.

Zambia

Some small-scale farmers had switched to other forms of earning income such as trading, charcoal production and brewing. The time of planting has changed and ridge and furrow techniques are adapted to save water.

Zimbabwe

The most common adaptation strategies are dry and early planting, which implies access to seed varieties that can stay in the soil for some time before the rains as well as very early- and short-maturing varieties. In addition there is also a great need for easy accessibility and availability of seasonal climatic forecasts of the oncoming season. Many farmers also use winter plowing and planting short-season varieties, use irrigation and grow drought resistant crops. Winter ploughing is very important as it helps conserve moisture, especially when it is done soon after the winter rains. But winter plowing necessitates access to draught power to carry out winter plowing in time. Because of the reliance on seeds with special characteristics, the disconnect between farmers and seed companies, research units and the government to ensure the availability of short-season and drought resistant crop varieties may be a barrier to adaptation. For example, very short-season maize varieties, such as SC401 and SC403, and medium varieties, like SC501, have been developed but are not being used in the affected regions.

Policy implications from the analyses of impacts on crop water requirements

The continent-wide comparison of crop water requirements indicates the huge variation in both the crop water use and the yield per unit of land and water. Having such variation across the continent explains the differences in area under maize in the different countries. More important, use of such information could be critical in policy decisions at the regional level. Having relative advantages for certain crops in certain countries or regions within a country could be taken into account in a supra continent accord for specialization and allocation of production quotas across countries. We will get back to this point in the policy discussion in the 'Policy implications' and 'Conclusions' sections of this chapter.

As was indicated earlier, there are several policy implications that can be drawn from the regional analysis of CROPWAT and Crop Water with Climate Change (CROPWATCC). First, it is clear that there are location-specific conditions that affect the performance of agricultural crops. Second, technological adjustment is key in adapting to climate in the various locations. It appears from the CROPWAT analyses that irrigation allows farmers to adapt much better, where water is available. The financial/economic aspects have to be further discussed (and this is done in the economic analysis in Chapter 5), but clearly irrigation provides higher yields that may justify the investment in irrigation. And third, the CO_2 fertilization effect, if correctly incorporated into the analysis, may turn the negative impact of climate change into a positive one by both shortening the growing season and reducing the water requirements of crops. By careful design of the incentive system for both technology adoption and location selection for certain crops, governments could enhance food production and reduce water use even under the severe climatic conditions in Africa.

Policy implications of farmers' reported adaptation strategies and barriers to adaptation

There are very marked differences in the ability of farmers from different countries to respond to change in climate. Farmers in Burkina Faso are much less likely to respond whereas farmers in Egypt almost invariably respond. The precise reasons underlying such differences could not be verified from the available data. They may be related to the quality of institutions, the existence of infrastructure, differences in prices or simply a manifestation of the way in which the survey was conducted and the data input.

An important policy question is whether agricultural adaptation in the face of climate can be expected to occur autonomously or whether government has a role in intervening. The results of this study make it clear that at least some adaptation takes place autonomously. For all sample countries, we found that governments could have an important role in promoting certain aspects.

Policy implications from river-basin hydrology modelling

The policy implications are serious and important to address. They include both the spatial and inter-temporal variability in stream flow. First, spatial variability across the continent is already big in the base period but it will increase with climate change in 2050 and become even larger in 2100. Second, both the low and the high ranges of inter-temporal flow will widen, introducing both frequent droughts and floods in many African countries. Bracing for these likely events by introducing adaptation measures earlier rather than later should become a priority of the governments and development agencies. Further, coordination among riparian states sharing the same basins should address both water management and dam operations to allow smoothing extreme events when they strike.

Policy implications from cross sectional regional adaptation

The regional analyses provide powerful tools that allow better understanding of farmers' behaviour when it comes to adaptation of crops, livestock and irrigation.

Crop choice

The results strongly suggest that adaptation policies to climate change must take into account crop selection. Treating crop choice as exogenous will seriously overestimate the damages from global warming. For example, agronomic studies or empirical studies that use weather as a proxy must be careful not to assume crop choices are exogenous. Farmers will probably change crops in response to a new climate rather than repeatedly grow crops that historically were successful but now fail. As a result, farmers will match future crops to future climates. Further, there is an important role for agronomic research in developing new varieties more suited for higher temperatures. Future farmers may have even better adaptation alternatives with an expanded set of crop choices specifically targeted at higher temperatures. Although this may still entail losses in agricultural income in Africa, the predicted losses will be much smaller than if farmers are limited to their current set of choices.

Livestock choice

Farmers in Africa will adapt to warming by slowly moving towards livestock management. Managing livestock in Africa is likely to be relatively more profitable than crops in future climate conditions. However, the mix of species chosen will be slightly different than today, with less emphasis on cattle and chickens and more on goats and sheep. These changes may be especially hard on larger farms that currently specialize in cattle. Although we anticipate that there will be widespread adaptations for small farmers, farmers should be able to make these transitions if climate change unfolds gradually and they are suitably advised by husbandry experts in extension services.

The analysis suggests that farmers just south of the Sahara will switch species, diversify their portfolio of animals, and move away from cattle and towards sheep. Small farmers will be able to make these changes without much change in expected net income. In contrast, large sheep farmers in South Africa may have to abandon sheep. These changes are predicted to reduce the net incomes of large farms considerably. African policy makers must be careful to encourage private adaptation during this period of change. There may be nothing that can be done to sustain the large cattle operations that depend on current climate. Providing subsidies or other enticements for such operations to continue once the climate changes would only compound the problem. Instead, governments should encourage farmers to change the composition of animals on their farms as needed. That is, they should inform farmers about how other livestock owners have coped with higher temperatures and share indigenous knowledge. Governments should anticipate that farmers will make changes on their lands and do whatever is needed to facilitate these changes.

Irrigation choice

Irrigation is an effective adaptation against reduction in rainfall and higher temperatures provided there is sufficient water available. This will be an effective remedy in select regions of Africa with water. However, for many regions, there is no available surface water, so that warming scenarios with reduced rainfall are particularly deleterious.

Conclusions

Policy makers may want to pay special attention to several successful adaptation practices. One adaptation that has moved very slowly in Africa is technology adoption. Africa lags behind the rest of the world in adopting irrigation, capital, and high-yield varieties (Evenson and Gollin, 2003). Some technologies may help farmers adapt to drier or hotter conditions, such as the development of new soybean varieties in Brazil. However, even climate-neutral technical advances will help farmers increase productivity and counterbalance losses from climate change. Through research and outreach, governments could encourage the development and use of varieties with more tolerance for the hot and dry conditions of many of Africa's agroclimatic zones. Diversification of crops, varieties and animal types, and practices based on comparative agroclimatic and economic advantage remain key adaptation measures.

The quantitative results suggest that promoting irrigation and mixed crop–livestock systems could help alleviate the likely effects of climate change in Africa, which were found to be sizeable under rainfed and sole cropping conditions. Where water is available, moving from rainfed to irrigated agriculture would increase not only average net revenue per hectare but also the resilience of agriculture to climate change. Governments could make public investments in infrastructure (Kurukulasuriya et al, 2006) and canals for water storage and conveyance where appropriate and where the public-good nature of these investments prevents adequate private sector investment. Investment in successful irrigation in sub-Saharan Africa ranges between $3600 and $5700 a hectare in 2000 prices (Inocencio et al, 2007). This analysis suggests that the difference between rainfed and irrigated agriculture runs between $150 and $5000 a hectare, depending on the country. This range of investment values implies that farmers in some countries could repay irrigation investments within a very reasonable period. Policy makers may want to consider supporting such coping interventions for climate change, where appropriate.

There are many country-specific differences in the propensity of individuals to adapt, and further analysis would be required to understand underlying factors. Adaptation, however, is something undertaken only by those who perceive climate change. The perception of climate change appears to hinge on farmer experience and the availability of extension advice specifically related to climate change. But while the policy options for promoting an increased awareness of climate change are more limited, earlier analysis indicates that the perception of climate change is already high.

In terms of policy implications it appears that enhanced farmer education would do most to hasten adaptation. More effective provision of extension advice may also play a role in promoting adaptation. In so far as distance to the selling market is a significant determinant of whether a farmer adapts to climate change, it may be that improved transport links would improve adaptation, although the precise mechanism underlying this is unclear. Better roads may allow farmers to switch from subsistence farming to cash crops, or facilitate the exchange of ideas through more regular trips to the market.

Notes

1. The reader is reminded that the Crop Water (CROPWAT) analyses may not be representative ones in the sense that both the crops and the regions selected do not provide an appropriate coverage of the various conditions (soil, climate, technologies, etc.). However, the results of reduction in crop production and increased water needs follow national trends in the countries where such analyses were performed.
2. While our sample includes several countries where relatively higher percentages of farmers were less concerned by changes in climate change (temperature and precipitation), no one country includes perceptions that either precipitation or temperature has not changed.

References

Adams, R. M., McCarl, B. A. and others (1998) 'Climate change and U.S. agriculture: Some further evidence', Report prepared for the Electric Power Research Institute as part of the Agricultural Impacts Project of the Climate Change Impacts Program (CCIP)

Alemayehu, M. (1998) 'Natural pasture improvement study smallholder dairy areas', Ministry of Agriculture (MoA) Small Dairy Development Project (SDDP), Addis Ababa

Alemayehu, M. (2003) *Ethiopia: Country Pasture/Forage Resource Profile*, Food and Agriculture Organization (FAO), Rome, www.fao.org/ag/agp/agpc/doc/counprof/ethiopia/ethiopia.htm

Bardhan, P. and Udry, C. (1999) *Development Microeconomics*, Oxford University Press, Oxford

Basist, A., Williams, C. N., Grody, N., Ross, T. and Shen, S. (2001) 'Using the special sensor microwave imager to monitor surface wetness', *Journal of Hydrometeorology* 2(3): 297–308

Benhin, J. K. A. (2006) 'Climate change and South African agriculture: Impacts and adaptation options', Discussion Paper (DP)21, Centre for Environmental Economics and Policy for Africa (CEEPA), University of Pretoria, South Africa

Benneh, G., Agyepong, G. T. and Allotey, J. A. (1990) *Land Degradation in Ghana*, Food Production and Rural Development Division, Commonwealth Secretariat, London

Benson, C. and Clay, E. (1998) 'The impact of drought on sub-Saharan economies', *World Bank Technical Paper 401*, World Bank, Washington DC

Boateng, E. (1998) 'Proceedings of workshop on land use planning', FAO Land Use Planning Project, TCP/GHA/6715/A

Boer G., Flato G. and Ramsden D. (2000) 'A transient climate change simulation with greenhouse gas and aerosol forcing: Projected climate for the 21st century', *Climate Dynamics* 16: 427–450

Burton, I. (2001) *Vulnerability and Adaptation to Climate Change in the Drylands*, The Global Drylands Partnership, Washington DC

Cline, W. (1996) 'The impact of global warming on agriculture: Comment', *American Journal of Agricultural Economics* 77: 1309–1312

Crosson, P. (1997) 'Impacts of climate change on agriculture', *Climate Issue Brief*, Resources For Future, no. 4

CSA (Central Statistics Authority) (1998) *Agricultural Survey of Farm Management Practises*, CSA, Addis Ababa

De Haan, A. (1999) 'Livelihoods and poverty: The role of migration – A critical review of the migration literature', *Journal of Development Studies* 36(2): 1–47

Deressa, T. T. (2006) 'Measuring the economic impact of climate change on Ethiopian agriculture: Ricardian approach', CEEPA DP25, University of Pretoria, South Africa

Desanker, P. V. (2002) *Impact of Climate Change on Africa*. Center for African Development Solutions, Johannesburg, South Africa, and University of Virginia, Charlottesville, VA.

Diop, M. (2006) 'Analysis of crop water use in Senegal with the CROPWAT model', CEEPA DP34, University of Pretoria, South Africa.

Doorenbos, J. and Kassam, A. H. (1977) 'Yield response to water', Irrigation and Drainage Paper 33, FAO, Rome

Downing, T. E. (1992) 'Climate change and vulnerable places: Global food security and country studies in Zimbabwe, Kenya, Senegal, and Chile', Research Paper No. 1, Environmental Change Unit, University of Oxford, Oxford, 54pp

Downing, T. E., Ringius, L., Hulme, M. and Waughray, D. (1997). 'Adapting to climate change in Africa', *Mitigation and Adaptation Strategies for Global Change* 2(1): 19–44

Durand, W. (2006) 'Assessing the impact of climate change on crop water use in South Africa', CEEPA DP28, University of Pretoria, South Africa

Eid, H. M. (1994) 'Impact of climate change on simulated wheat and maize yields in Egypt', in Rosenzweig, C. and Iglesias, A. (eds) *Implications of Climate Change for International Agriculture: Crop Modeling Study*, US Environmental Protection Agency, Washington DC

Eid, H. M., El-Marsafawy, S. M. and Samiha, A. O. (2006) 'Assessing the economic impacts of climate change on agriculture in Egypt: A Ricardian approach', CEEPA DP16, University of Pretoria, South Africa

El-Shaer, M. H., Eid, H. M., Rosenzweig, C., Iglesias, A. and Hillel, D. (1996) 'Agricultural adaptation to climate change in Egypt', in Smith, J., Bhatti, N., Menzhulin, G., Benioff, R., Budyko, M. I., Campos, M., Jallow, B. and Rijsberman, F. (eds) *Adapting to Climate Change: An International Perspective*, Springer-Verlag, New York

Emori, S., Nozawa, T., Abe-Ouchi, A., Namaguti, A. and Kimoto, M. (1999) 'Coupled ocean-atmosphere model experiments of future climate change with an explicit representation of sulfate aerosol scattering', *Journal of the Meteorological Society of Japan* 77: 1299–1307

Evenson, R. and Gollin, D. (2003) 'Crop genetic improvement in developing countries: Overview and summary', in Evenson, R. and Gollin, D. (eds) *Crop Variety Improvement and its Effect on Productivity: The Impact of International Agricultural Research*, Cabi Publishing, Wallington, 1–38

Fafchamps, M. (1999) *Rural Poverty, Risk, and Development*. Report submitted to the FAO. Centre for the Study of African Economies, Oxford University, Oxford

FAO (1984a) *Agroclimatic Resource Inventory for Land Use Planning, Ethiopia*, Technical Report 2, AG: DP/ETH/78/003, FAO, Rome

FAO (1984b) *Assistance to Land Use Planning in Ethiopia. Land Use, Production Regions and Farming Systems Inventory*, Technical Report 3, AG: DP/ETH/78/003, FAO, Rome

FAO (1993) 'CROPWAT, a computer program for irrigation planning and management' (by Martin Smith), Irrigation and Drainage Paper 46, FAO, Rome

FAO (2000) *The State Of Food and Agriculture 2000*, FAO, Rome

FAO (2001) *Food and Agriculture Organisation of the United Nations/Global Information and Early Warning System on Food and Agriculture (FAO/GIEWS)*, (http://www.fao.org/giews/english/basedocs/saf.htm)

FAO (2003) *The Digital Soil Map of the World*, version 3.6 (January), FAO, Rome

FAO (2006) 'Republic of Senegal (case study)', online sourcebook on decentralization and local development, CIESIN, Columbia University, www.ciesin.org/decentralization/Entryway/english-contents.html

Fischer, G. and Van Velthuizen, H. T. (1996) *Climate Change and Global Agricultural Potential Project: A Case Study of Kenya*, International Institute for Applied Systems Analysis, Laxenburg, Austria, 96pp

Gambiza, J. and Nyama, C. (2000) *Zimbabwe: Country Pasture/Forage Resource Profile*, FAO, Rome http://www.fao.org/ag/agp/agpc/doc/counprof/zimbabwe/zimbab.htm

Geesing, D. and Djibo, H. (2001) *Niger: Country Pasture/Forage Resource Profile*, FAO, Rome http://www.fao.org/ag/agp/agpc/doc/counprof/ niger/niger.htm

Giorgis, K., Tadege, A. and Tibebe, D. (2006) 'Estimating crop water use and simulating yield reduction for maize and sorghum in Ddma and Miesso districts using the CROPWAT model', CEEPA DP31, University of Pretoria, South Africa

Government of the Republic of Senegal (1997) Senegalese Government's Initial Communication on Climate Change

Hernes, H., Dalfelt, A., Berntsen, T., Holtsmark, B., Otto, L., Selrod, R. and Aaheim, H. A. (1995) *Climate Strategy for Africa*, Center for International Climate and Environmental Research, University of Oslo

Hess, U. and Syroka, H. (2005) *Weather-based Insurance in Southern Africa. The Case of Malawi*, Agriculture and Rural Development (ARD) Discussion Paper 13, World Bank, Washington DC

Houghton J. T. et al (eds) (2001) 'Climate change 2001: The scientific basis', contribution of Working Group I to the third assessment report of the Intergovernmental Panel on Climate Change (IPCC), Cambridge University Press, Cambridge http://edcdaac.usgs.gov/ gtopo30/gtopo30.asp

Hulme, M. (ed.) (1996) *Climate Change and Southern Africa*. Climatic Research Unit, University of East Anglia, Norwich, 104pp

Hulme, M., Doherty, R., Ngara, T., New, M. and Lister, D. (1999) 'African climate change: 1900-2100', *Climate Research* 17: 145–168

Inocencio, A., Kikuchi, M., Tonosaki, M., Maruyama, A., Merrey, D., Sally, H. and de Jong, I. (2007) *Costs and Performance of Irrigation Projects: A Comparison of Sub-Saharan Africa and Other Developing Regions*, IWMI Research Report 109, http://www.iwmi.cgiar.org/pubs/PUB109/RR109-final.pdf

IPCC (2001) *Climate Change 2001: Impacts, Adaptation and Vulnerability*, Cambridge University Press, Cambridge

IPCC (1996) 'Impacts, adaptations, and mitigation of climate change: Scientific-technical analyses', Contribution of Working Group II to the IPCC Second Assessment Report, Cambridge University Press, Cambridge

IPCC (2007) *Climate Change 2007: The Physical Science Basis*, Contribution of Working Group I to the Fourth Assessment Report of the IPCC, Cambridge University Press, Cambridge

Jain, S. (2006) 'An empirical economic assessment of impacts of climate change on agriculture in Zambia', CEEPA DP27, University of Pretoria, South Africa

Jolly, C. M., Kusumastanto, T., Sissoko, M. M. and Olowolayemo, S. (1995) *The Effects of Climate Change on Senegal's Agricultural Sector*, Cooperative Agreement, US Department of Agriculture, Economics Research Service, Washington DC

Kabubo-Mariara, J. and Karanja, F. K. (2006) 'The economic impact of climate change on Kenyan crop agriculture: A Ricardian approach', CEEPA DP12, University of Pretoria, South Africa

Karanja, F. K. (2006) 'CROPWAT model analysis of crop water use in six districts in Kenya', CEEPA DP35, University of Pretoria, South Africa

Kurukulasuriya, P. (2004) presentation at project workshop, kwazulu-Natal, South Africa, 3–6 May 2004

Kurukulasuriya, P. and Mendelsohn, R. (2006a) 'A Ricardian analysis of the impact of climate change on African cropland', CEEPA DP8, University of Pretoria, South Africa

Kurukulasuriya, P. and Mendelsohn, R. (2006b) 'Endogenous irrigation: The impact of climate change on farmers in Africa', CEEPA DP18, University of Pretoria, South Africa

Kurukulasuriya, P. and Mendelsohn, R. (2006c) 'Crop selection: Adapting to climate change in Africa', CEEPA DP26, University of Pretoria, South Africa

Kurukulasuriya, P., Mendelsohn, R., Hassan, R., Benhin, J., Deressa, T., Diop, M., Eid, H. M., Yerfi Fosu, K., Gbetibouo, G., Jain, S., Mahamadou, A., Mano, R., Kabubo-Mariara, J., El-Marsafawy, S., Molua, E., Ouda, S., Ouedraogo, M., Sène, I., Maddison, D., Seo, N. and Dinar, A. (2006) 'Will African agriculture survive climate change?', *World Bank Economic Review* 20(3): 367–388

Kurukulasuriya, P. and Rosenthal, S. (2003) 'Climate change and agriculture: A review of impacts and adaptations', Environment Department Papers, Paper 91, World Bank, Washington DC, June

Lamousé-Smith, B. W. and School, J. (1998) *Africa Interaction Maps*, version 1, http://www.course.psu.edu/aaa_s/aaa_s110_tah/AFIM

Lotsch, A. (2006) 'Modeling drought hazards in Africa', CEEPA DP14, University of Pretoria, South Africa

Maddison, D., Manley, M. and Kurukulasuriya, P. (2006) 'The impact of climate change on African agriculture: A Ricardian approach', CEEPA DP15, University of Pretoria, South Africa

Magalhaes, A. (2000) 'Climate affairs in Latin America: Climate issues and policy responses', Paper presented at the Institute of Latin American Studies, Columbia University, 31 January to 2 February 2000, New York, NY

Maï Moussa, K. and Amadou, M. (2006) 'Using the Cropwat model to analyse the effects of climate change on rainfed crops in Niger', CEEPA DP32, University of Pretoria, South Africa

Makadho, J. M. (1996) 'Potential effects of climate change on corn production in Zimbabwe', *Climate Research* 6: 147–151

Mano, R. and Nhemachena, C. (2006) 'Assessment of the economic impacts of climate change on agriculture in Zimbabwe: A Ricardian approach', CEEPA DP11, University of Pretoria, South Africa

Matarira, C. H. and Mwamuka, F. C. (1996) 'Vulnerability of Zimbabwe forests to global climate change', *Climate Research* 6(2): 135–136

Mendelsohn, R. (1999) 'Efficient adaptation to climate change', *Climatic Change* 45: 583–600

Mendelsohn, R. (2000) 'Efficient adaptation to climate change', *Climatic Change*, 45: 583–600

Mendelsohn, R., Dinar, A. and Dalfelt, A. (2000) *Climate Change Impacts on African Agriculture*, World Bank, Washington DC (Mimeo)

Mendelsohn, R., Kurukulasuriya, P., Basist, A., Kogan, F. and Williams, C. (2007) 'Climate analysis with satellite versus ground station data', *Climatic Change* 81(1): 71–83

Mendelsohn R. and Neumann, J. (eds) (1999) *The Impacts of Climate Change on the U.S. Economy*, Cambridge University Press, Cambridge

Mendelsohn, R., Nordhaus, W. D. and Shaw, D. (1994) 'The impact of global warming on agriculture: A Ricardian analysis', *American Economic Review* 84(4): 753–771

Mendelsohn, R., Nordhaus, W. D. and Shaw, D. (1996) 'Climate impacts on aggregate farm value: Accounting for adaptation', *Agricultural and Forest Meteorology* 80: 55–66

Ministry of Agriculture (MoA) (2000) *Agroecological Zonations of Ethiopia*, MoA, Addis Ababa

Ministry of Food and Agriculture (MoFA) (1998) *National Soil Fertility Management Action Plan*, Directorate of Crop Services, Accra

Molua, E. L. and Lambi, C. M. (2006a) 'Climate, hydrology and water resources in Cameroon', CEEPA DP33, University of Pretoria, South Africa

Molua, E. L. and Lambi, C. M. (2006b) 'The economic impact of climate change on agriculture in Cameroon', CEEPA DP17, University of Pretoria, South Africa

Mortimore, M. J. and Adams, W. M. (2000) 'Farmer adaptation, change and crisis in the Sahel', *Global Environmental Change* 11: 49–57

Moussa, K. M. and Amadou, M. (2006) 'Using the CROPWAT model to analyse the effects of climate change on rainfed crops in Niger', CEEPA DP32, University of Pretoria, South Africa

Muchena, P. (1994) 'Implications of climate change for maize yields in Zimbabwe', in Rosenzweig, C. and Iglesias, A. (eds) *Implications of Climate Change for International Agriculture: Crop Modeling Study*, US Environmental Protection Agency, Washington DC

National Department of Agriculture (2001a) Abstract of Agricultural Statistics, Directorate, Agricultural Information, NDA, Pretoria

National Department of Agriculture (2001b) *Agricultural Digest 2000/2001*, NDA, Pretoria

O'Brien, K., Sygna, L., Næss, L. O., Kingamkono, R. and Hochobeb, B. (2000) 'Is information enough? User responses to seasonal climate forecasts in Southern Africa', Report 2000:3, Center for International Climate and Environmental Research (CICERO), Oslo

OFDA/CRED International Disaster Database (http://www.cred.be/emdat)

Onyeji, S. C. and Fischer, G. (1994) 'An economic analysis of potential impacts of climate change in Egypt', *Global Environmental Change and Policy Dimensions* 4(4): 281–299

Oppong-Anane, K. (2001) *Ghana: Country Pasture/Forage Resource Profile*, Food and Agriculture Organization, Rome http://www.fao.org/ag/agp/agpc/doc/counprof/ghana/ghana.htm

Orodho, A. B. (2001) *Kenya: Country Pasture/Forage Resource Profile*, Food and Agriculture Organization, Rome http://www.fao.org/ag/agp/agpc/doc/counprof/kenya/kenya.htm

Ouedraogo, M., Some, L. and Dembele, Y. (2006a) 'Economic impact assessment of climate change on agriculture in Burkina Faso: A Ricardian approach', CEEPA DP24, University of Pretoria, South Africa

Ouedraogo, M., Some, L. and Dembele, Y. (2006b) 'Ricardian impact assessment: Case study of Burkina Faso', a report submitted to the CEEPA in Africa, University of Pretoria, as part of a GEF/WB study on 'Regional Climate, Water and Agriculture: Impacts on and Adaptation of Agro-ecological Systems in Africa' (unpublished)

Palmer, T. and Ainslie, A. (2002) *South Africa: Country Pasture/Forage Resource Profile*, FAO, Rome http://www.fao.org/ag/agp/agpc/doc/counprof/southafrica/southafrica.htm

Pélissier, P. (1983) 'L'agriculture', in *Atlas du Sénégal*, 2ème éd., Jeune Afrique, Paris

Phillips, J. and McIntyre, B. (2000) 'ENSO and interannual rainfall variability in Uganda: Implications for agricultural management', *International Journal of Climatology* 20(2): 171–182

Poonyth, D., Hassan, R. M., Gbetibouo, G. A., Ramaila, J. M. and Letsoalo, M. A. (2002) 'Measuring the impact of climate change on South African agriculture: A Ricardian approach', Paper presented at the 40th Annual Agricultural Economics Association of South Africa Conference, Bloemfontein, 18–20 September

Rosenzweig, C. R., Parry, M. L. and Fischer, G. (1995) 'World food supply', in Strzepek, K. M. and Smith, J. B. (eds) *As Climate Changes: International Impacts and Implications,* Cambridge University Press, Cambridge

Schlesinger, M. E. and Zhao, Z. C. (1989) 'Seasonal climate changes induced by doubled CO_2 as simulated by the OSU atmospheric GCM/mixed layer ocean model', *Climate* 2: 459–495

Schulze, R. E. (1997) *South African Atlas of Agrohydrology and Climatology*, Report TT82/96, Water Research Commission, Pretoria

Schulze, R. E., Kiker, G. A. and Kunz, R. P. (1993) 'Global climate change and agricultural productivity in southern Africa', *Global Environmental Change* 3(4): 330–349

Schulze, R., Kiker, G. and Kunz, R. P. (1996) 'Global climate change and agricultural productivity in southern Africa: Thought for food and food for thought', in Downing, T. (ed.) *Climate Change and World Food Security*, North Atlantic Treaty Organisation ASI Series, Volume 137, Springer-Verlag, Berlin and Heidelberg, 421–447

Schulze, R. E., Maharaj, M., Lynch, S. D., Howe, B. J. and Melvile-Thomson, B. (2001) *South African Atlas of Agrohydrology and Climatology*, Digital Atlas Beta version 1.002, Department of Agricultural Engineering, University of Natal, South Africa

Sene, I. M., Diop, M. and Dieng, A. (2006) 'Impacts of climate change on the revenues and adaptation of farmers in Senegal', CEEPA DP20, University of Pretoria, South Africa

Seo, N. and Mendelsohn, R. (2006a) 'Climate change impacts on animal husbandry in Africa: A Ricardian analysis', CEEPA DP9, University of Pretoria, South Africa

Seo, N. and Mendelsohn, R. (2006b) 'The impact of climate change on livestock management in Africa: A structural Ricardian analysis', CEEPA DP23, University of Pretoria, South Africa

Seo, N. and Mendelsohn, R. (2006c) 'Climate change adaptation in Africa: A microeconomic analysis of livestock choice', CEEPA DP19 University of Pretoria, South Africa

Sivakumar, M. (1992) 'Climate change and implications for agriculture in Niger', *Climate Change* 20: 297–312

Skees, J. R., Gober, S., Varangis, P., Lester, R. and Kalavakonda, V. (2002) 'Developing rainfall-based index insurance in Morocco', Working Paper 2577, World Bank, Washington DC

Sombroek, W. G., Braun, H. M. H. and Van der Pow, B. J. A. (1982) 'Exploratory soil map and agro-climatic zone map of Kenya' (scale: 1:100,000), Report No. E1, Kenya Soil Survey, Nairobi

Some, L., Dembele, Y., Ouedraogo, M., Some, B., Kambire, F. and Sangare, S. (2006) 'Analysis of crop water use and soil water balance in Burkina Faso using Cropwat', CEEPA DP36, University of Pretoria, South Africa

Statistics, Research and Information Directorate (SRID) (2001) *Agriculture in Ghana: Facts and Figures*, MoFA, Accra

Strzepek, K. and McClusky, A. (2006) 'District level hydroclimatic time series and scenario analysis to assess the impacts of climatic change on regional water resources and agriculture in Africa', CEEPA DP13, University of Pretoria, South Africa

Strzepek, K. and Smith, J. B. (eds) (1995) *As Climate Changes: International Impacts and Implications*, Cambridge University Press, Cambridge

Thompson, S. L. and Pollard, D. (1995) 'A global climate model (GENESIS) with a land-surface-transfer scheme (LSX). Part 1: Present-day climate', *Journal of Climate* 8: 732–761

Tyson, P. D., Lee-Thorp, J., Holmgren, K. and Thackeray, J. F. (2002) 'Changing gradients of climate change in southern Africa during the past millennium: Implications for population movements', *Climatic Change* 52: 129–135

Udry, C. (1990) 'Credit markets in northern Nigeria: Credit as insurance in a rural economy', *World Bank Economic Review* 4(3): 251–269

United States Geological Survey (USGS) (2004) Global 30 Arc Second Elevation Data, USGS National Mapping Division, EROS Data Centre

USAID (2006) *Geography of Senegal*, http://edcintl.cr.usgs.gov/senegal2/veg.html

Vincent, V. and Thomas, R. G. (1960) *An Agricultural Survey of Southern Rhodesia. Part I: Agro-ecological Survey*, Government Printer, Salisbury

Wahaj, R., Maraux, F. and Munoz, G. (2006) 'Actual crop water use in project countries: A synthesis at the regional level', CEEPA DP38, University of Pretoria, South Africa

Washington, W. M., Weatherly, J. W., Meehl, G. A., Semtner Jr, A. J., Bettge, T. W., Craig, A. P., Strand Jr, W. G., Arblaster, J. M., Wayland, V. B., James, R. and Zhang, Y. (2000) 'Parallel climate model (PCM): Control and transient scenarios', *Climate Dynamics* 16: 755–774

Weng, F. and Grody, N. (1998) 'Physical retrieval of land surface temperature using the Special Sensor Microwave Imager', *Journal of Geophysical Research* 103: 8839–8848

World Bank (2003) 'Africa rainfall and temperature evaluation system (ARTES)', World Bank, Washington DC

World Bank (2005) *Managing Agricultural Production Risk*, Report 32727-GLB, ARD Department, World Bank, Washington DC

Yates, D. (1997) 'Approaches to continental scale runoff for integrated assessment models', *Journal of Hydrology* 201: 289–310

Yates, D. N. and Strzepek, K. M. (1998) 'Modeling the nile basin under climate change', *Journal of Hydrologic Engineering* 3(2): 98–108

Annex 1

Literature Review on Adaptation in Africa

The following brief literature review is based to a large extent on a more in depth review by Kurukulasuriya and Rosenthal, 2003. It provides the reader with some supporting evidence based on existing work on impact of and adaptation to climate change in agriculture in Africa.

Background

The concern with climate change is heightened given the linkage of the agriculture sector to poverty. It is anticipated that adverse impacts on the agriculture sector will exacerbate the incidence of rural poverty. Impact costs are going to be particularly severe in developing countries where the agriculture sector is an important source of livelihood. In Africa, estimates indicate that nearly 60–70 per cent of the population is dependent on the agriculture sector for employment, and the sector contributes on average nearly 34 per cent to gross domestic product (GDP) per country.[1] With lower technological and capital stocks, the agriculture sector in such poorer developing countries is especially unlikely to withstand the additional pressures imposed by climate change without a concerted response strategy (Crosson, 1997). According to some estimates, the overall economic impact of climate change on the agriculture sector could be up to 10 per cent of GDP (Hernes et al, 1995; Intergovernmental Panel on Climate Change (IPCC), 2001).

Mechanism for climate impact on crops

Temperatures in Africa are expected to rise at less than the global average, and will have varying impacts depending upon the underlying type of agro-ecological zone. That is, impacts will depend on initial temperatures. Fischer and Van Velthuizen (1996) and Downing (1992) explore the impact of climate change on Kenya, and find that higher temperatures would have a positive impact in highland areas. Downing (1992), relying on a model of land use to estimate changes in availability of land suitable for cropping, has shown that in highland areas of western Kenya, there is likely to be a 67 per cent increase in 'high potential' land in response to a 2.5°C rise in average temperature. In contrast, rising ambient temperatures may have a detrimental effect in many lowland areas, particularly those that are semi-arid. For some crops, plant metabolism begins to break down above 40°C. Reduction in growing periods due to accelerated growth can reduce the yields (Hulme, 1996).

Water availability (or runoff) is a critical factor in determining the impact of climate change in many places, particularly in Africa. A number of studies suggest that precipitation and the length of the growing season are critical in determining whether climate change positively or negatively affects agriculture (Sivakumar, 1992; Strzepek and Smith, 1995; Fischer and Van Velthuizen, 1996; Hulme, 1996). However, as outlined earlier, limited scientific ability to predict trends in rainfall with much certainty is of particular concern for areas such as southern Africa where El Niño-Southern Oscillation (ENSO) effects are considered to be important. For other parts of the continent too, there is less confidence about precipitation than other climatic changes. A lack of comprehensive regional and sub-regional climate models and sufficient country-level impact studies limits researchers' abilities to reach firm conclusions about related impacts on agriculture and their economic values.

The expected variability of temperature, precipitation, atmospheric carbon content and extreme events are forecast to have profound effects on plant growth and yields, crops, soils, insects, weed, diseases, livestock and water availability in Africa (Adams et al, 1998; see also IPCC (1996) for a wide-ranging overview of the likely impacts on the agriculture sector). Burton (2001) suggests that expected impacts in dryland areas include reduction in rainfall, rise in temperature, and increased rainfall variability. Some areas may even get higher levels of rainfall, such as in arid areas including Mauritania, Mali and Niger. Highland areas are also expected to benefit, since the growing season would be lengthened and the incidence of frost diminished. In contrast, other, more sub-humid, zones of Burkina Faso, Mali and Ghana are expected to suffer from reductions in rainfall.

Agronomic and agro-ecological zone analysis studies

A number of publications (Downing, 1992; Rosenzweig et al, 1995; Desanker, 2002) focus on the 'vulnerability' of African countries to climate induced reductions in agricultural production, and on the impact on individual farmers. Downing (1992) examines the impact of climate change on food security in three countries in Africa (Zimbabwe, Kenya and Senegal). A variety of methods is employed, and careful attention is given to the definition of vulnerability. Data on numerous non-climatic factors such as the socio-economic setting, trade issues, institutional structures and geography are drawn on to examine 'current vulnerability, risk of present and future climatic variations and responses to reduce present vulnerability and improve resiliency to future risks'.

Hulme et al (1999) examine actual and predicted continent-wide changes in temperature and rainfall in Africa during 1900–2100, drawing on data related to diurnal temperature range and rainfall variability. Using emissions scenarios prepared for the IPCC Third Assessment Report and other models, the study presents four new scenarios, or 'futures', of regional temperature, rainfall, CO_2 concentrations and sea-level changes. The results of the scenarios are consistent with the IPCC conclusion, indicating that warming will continue and in most cases will accelerate. While the authors assert that in 100 years the continent could be 2–6°C warmer on average, they are less confident about future changes in rainfall, due to two primary reasons. Firstly, ENSO-type climate variability, a key determinant of rainfall variability in Africa, has not been represented satisfactorily in most global climate change models. In addition, the failure of general circulation models (GCMs) to account for dynamic land cover–atmosphere interaction and dust and biomass aerosols, important interactions in explaining climate variability, including recent desiccation of the Sahel region, reduce the confidence of estimates on future precipitation levels.

Research on the agronomic impacts of climate change in Africa has largely focused on southern Africa. Hulme (1996) describes three models for maize that have been used for impact analysis in this region. The Crop Estimation through Resource and Environment Synthesis- (CERES-) maize site model was used to examine sites in Zimbabwe. Research reported in publications by Eid (1994), Muchena (1994) and Makadho (1996) is based on this model. The Agrohydrological Model of the Agricultural Catchments Research Unit (ACRU) with CERES-maize is described in Schulze et al (1993) and Schulze et al (1996). Finally, the monthly crop-climate model uses the Food and Agriculture Organization (FAO) water requirements satisfaction index (WRSI) to assess the sensitivity of maize to moisture deficits at certain times of year. Conclusions from these studies appear to be consistent. In most areas of southern Africa, the benefits from increases in CO_2 (higher water-use efficiency, higher rates of photosynthesis) would outweigh adverse effects of lower rainfall and higher temperatures. The window for planting is also lengthened, which can have a positive effect. This research is applied in a number of country- and region-specific studies of the wider impacts of climate change, which are described in publications reviewed further below.

Sivakumar (1992) focuses on changing rainfall patterns and production of pearl millet, the main staple crop in Niger. He finds that the monthly data used in previous studies on the implications of declining rainfall for agriculture in western Africa was too arbitrary to be a realistic index of crop responses. Using data on daily precipitation from 21 stations from the Niger rainfall database at the International Crops Research Institute for the Semi-Arid Tropics (ICRISAT)

Sahelian Center, the author establishes patterns over the period 1921–1990 and explores correlations with millet yields and aggregate production. His conclusions indicate that shifts in the patterns of rainfall during the 1965–1988 period (relative to the 1945–1965 period), reduced the growing season by 5–20 days across various locations in Niger, making cropping more risky. Sivakumar notes that the implications for agriculture are important, not only because the absolute amount of rainfall has decreased, but also because its timing has changed. In particular, a decrease in the August rainfall is troubling for millet producers because of the lack of adequate water supply during the sensitive reproductive growth stage. The author notes that in times of drought farmers will sacrifice cash crops in order to save food crops; a finding that may partially explain a decline in groundnut production over a 10–15 year period beginning in the mid-1960s. This type of climatic change is thought to have important implications for sustainable agriculture, since continuing low rainfall may result in accelerated environmental degradation. A failure to intensify production has led to cropping in marginal lands that are more susceptible to rainfall variability and wind erosion.

Other publications reporting on research in Africa apply agronomic research to investigations of the wider impacts of climate change for a particular country or region. These include Phillips and McIntyre (2000) on Uganda, Fischer and van Velthuizen (1996) on Kenya, Schulze et al (1993) on southern Africa and Makadho (1996) on Zimbabwe.

According to Downing's outlook for Kenya in 1992, potential food production would increase with higher temperatures and greater rainfall. However, those in semi-arid areas, particularly 'vulnerable socio-economic groups', could face serious difficulties when their already low yields decrease further as a result of insufficient rainfall. Similarly, Fischer and Van Velthuizen (1996) suggest that the overall impact on the sector may be positive, but that results will vary by region. Kenya has a wide range of agro-ecological conditions, from hot and arid lowland areas to cool humid highlands. Increases in concentrations of CO_2 are expected to have a positive effect overall, as would additional rainfall, to the extent they occur. The authors warn, however, that if rising temperatures are not accompanied by increases in precipitation (to make up for higher rates of evapotranspiration) then large decreases in agricultural production could result. This is a particular concern in low lying areas of eastern and southern Kenya. In the highlands of the central and western parts of the country, higher temperatures could increase production due to larger areas becoming suitable for cropping. Furthermore, due to higher cropping intensities in these places, higher production would more than outweigh any effects of lower moisture. In some areas, reduced moisture could diminish the potential impact of pests and disease. The authors conclude that 'national level food productivity potential of Kenya may well increase with higher levels of atmospheric carbon dioxide and climate change induced increases in temperature, provided this is accompanied by some increase in precipitation as predicted by several global circulation models'.

Makadho (1996) shows this to be a likely outcome for maize in Zimbabwe, with decreasing yields of up to 17 per cent in drier areas. Using climate data from four agro-ecologically representative stations in Zimbabwe, the author based his analysis upon two climate change models Global Fluid Dynamics Laboratory (GFDL) and Climate and Carbon Cycle Modelling (CCCM). Under both irrigated and non-irrigated conditions, in some regions maize production is expected to decrease significantly (approximately by 11 to 17 per cent). Increments in temperature that consequently shorten the crop growth period, especially the 'grain-filling period' are underlined as the primary cause of the crop reductions.

Downing (1992) also confirms that shifts in agroclimatic potential would affect national food production and land use in Zimbabwe. With a 2°C increase in temperature, the core agricultural zone decreases by a third. The semi-extensive farming zone is particularly sensitive to small changes in climate. Farmers in this zone, already vulnerable in terms of self-sufficiency and food security, are expected to be further marginalized due to increased risk of crop failure. A subsequent report by the Government of Zimbabwe follows closely the analysis and results found in Downing (1992) and Hulme (1996).

The focus of the analysis for Senegal is on population growth in the face of climate change. A carrying capacity model is applied that compares consumption requirements with food production. The findings for 1990 suggest that, of the country's 93 arrondissements, two-thirds have rural populations exceeding their rainfed carrying capacity. While recognizing the limits of the model, the author believes these results should be of concern, particularly if climate change were to increase the number of areas that are not food self-sufficient.

The Senegalese Government's Initial Communication on Climate Change (Government of the Republic of Senegal, 1997), provides a detailed account of the same research reported in Downing (1992). The report devotes significant attention to the implications of climate change for food security, and emphasizes the pressure that a 2.7 per cent per annum population growth rate places on the economy in light of the climate change that has taken place since 1966 – mainly in the form of much reduced rainfall.

Hulme (1996) suggests that the droughts of 1984/85 and 1991/92 in southern Africa showed how vulnerable the southern Africa region is to climate and the impact that changes can have on food security and water resources. Both droughts had a significant impact on maize production in the southern Africa region. Problems of desertification are attributed more to human impacts, particularly demographic change. Moreover, analyses of vulnerability centre on national food balances, food production and dependence on food imports and food aid. Hulme (1996) also constructs an index of vulnerability based on these variables and gross national product (GNP), and rates eight countries. According to the model, South Africa is the least vulnerable and Angola is most vulnerable. Downing (1992) characterizes vulnerability as (i) referring to a consequence as opposed to a cause, (ii) implying an adverse consequence, and (iii) a 'relative term' rather than an absolute measurement of deprivation.

Yates and Strzepek (1998) explore how climate induced changes in water resource availability, crop yields, crop water use, land resources and global agricultural markets affect Egyptian agriculture. The authors point out the uniqueness of the agricultural sector in Egypt, namely that all agricultural land is irrigated with Nile river water. Although Egypt's population is not growing quickly as compared with many other developing countries, an expected doubling by 2060 requires efforts to increase agricultural production. The authors believe the country's high dependence on natural resources make it especially vulnerable to climate change.

The paper confirms previous suspicions that Egypt is vulnerable to global warming, fluctuations in agricultural markets (local and global), and changes in agriculture and water and land resources. Specific conclusions that are made include: (i) population and economic growth scenarios are significant factors; (ii) how a country adapts to climate change is important; (iii) water resources availability and crop water use are important to consider in assessing vulnerability; (iv) water is a limiting factor; (v) economic, trade and social policies greatly affect the potential integrated impacts of climate change. Finally, emphasis is placed on the value of an integrated, economy-wide approach to assessing impacts and vulnerability.

Benson and Clay (1998) explore the impact of droughts on national economies in southern Africa. Using data from countries including Namibia, Zimbabwe, South Africa, Mozambique, Malawi, Lesotho and Botswana, they maintain that more developed economies may be more vulnerable to such shocks than the less developed countries of Africa. While less developed economies would appear to be more vulnerable because of their dependence on agriculture, 'weak intersectoral linkages, a high degree of self-provisioning, relatively small nonagricultural sectors, and often poor transport infrastructure' have the effect of containing the impact of the drought. Evidence presented in the report suggests that the relationship between the level of complexity of an economy and its vulnerability to drought takes a hill-shaped form.

Estimates of impacts of climate change with adaptation

Numerous agronomic studies have focused on African countries. Muchena (1994) explored the impact of climate change on maize production in Zimbabwe, and in simulations found that a 2°C rise in ambient temperature led to unacceptably low yields. A similar result was observed even when the positive effects of a concomitant rise in CO_2 levels were included in the analysis. More recently, Phillips and McIntyre (2000) describe results from a study of historical climate data aimed at understanding the effect of ENSO events on agriculture in Uganda. They show that sea surface temperatures associated with these events bring about different changes in unimodal and bimodal rainfall areas. In unimodal zones, 'the El Niño events are associated with a depression of the August peak in rainfall, but a lengthening of the season, potentially providing an opportunity for growing later-maturing crops. In bimodal areas, there is little change in the first peak in August, but the second peak in November is enhanced in El Niño years and depressed in La Niña years'. The authors discuss implications for the choice of crops and the timing of planting, and point out that making use of this information may depend on the existence of an effective extension service. Cropping changes may require inputs of various types, such as fertilization.

Schulze et al (1993) apply the CERES-maize model used in a study of Zimbabwe, while Muchena (1994) and Makadho (1996) apply it to South Africa, Lesotho and Swaziland. The analysis simulates yields and productivity under present and future climatic conditions, taking into account the effects of increasing CO_2 concentrations and resultant expected increases in temperature. Changes in precipitation are not considered given the uncertainty of predicted changes. The results show a large dependence on the intra-seasonal and inter-annual variation of rainfall. Results from the primary productivity model indicate that a decline in productivity is likely to be marginal. Soil water availability is a key variable and accounts for a fair amount of geographic variability. Results from the yield analysis show that for nitrogen-unlimited simulations in areas yielding at least 8 tons/ha, elevated temperatures and CO_2 concentrations fail to increase yields significantly. In more variable conditions (4–8t/ha), there is an expansion of area into areas previously yielding below 4t/ha. In areas with marginal rainfall for maize production, climate change has little impact on the already low yields. Overall, the results point to a general increment in potential maize production.

Onyeji and Fischer (1994) consider the impacts of climate change on Egypt. They use estimates of potential changes in agricultural production under conditions of global climate change to provide insights on the economy-wide implications for Egypt. The analysis takes account of wider impacts of climate change on world commodity trade, and the consequent effect on Egypt's economy. The study examines scenarios with and without adaptation, and compares results with a reference scenario of no climate change.

Estimates of changing crop yields are centred on maize and wheat, based on the International Benchmarks Sites Network for Agrotechnology Transfer (IBSNAT) crop model simulation experiments at two sites in Egypt. The data are coupled with production data from the crop modellers, FAO and United States Department of Agriculture (USDA), to get changes in national yield. Yield changes for crops other than wheat and maize were estimated 'based on their similarities to the modeled crops'. Estimates were made for three scenarios under each of the Goddard Institute for Space Studies (GISS), GFDL and United Kingdom Meteorological Office (UKMO) models, with and without the effects of CO_2 enrichment. The first scenario assumes no investments in adaptation, the second only small investments, and the third large investments. The projected changes in yield were then applied to the Basic Linked System (BLS) of National Agricultural Models, a model developed by the International Institute for Applied Systems Analysis. Impacts for the period 1990–2060 were simulated. The BLS is a world-level general equilibrium model, with 35 national and regional models; individual models are linked via a world market module. Among the results, the authors find that large investments in adaptation are required to make significant gains in avoiding the adverse impacts on the economy. Changes in GDP range from –6.2 per cent (no adaptation) to +0.7 per cent (large investments in adaptation).

Adaptations to climate change

It is expected to see reactive or anticipatory adaptations. Reactive (or autonomous) adaptations consist of temporary coping strategies that agents and institutions are likely to make in response to climate change after the fact (ex-post). The effectiveness of reactive measures is thus dependent on resources at hand to cope with a sudden unexpected event (i.e. capacity to adapt autonomously, including institutional support, manpower, financial or technological resources, and confidence in the market, to name a few). But focusing policy on autonomous adaptation is likely to be futile because there is no guarantee that the necessary processes that trigger adaptation will occur. On the other hand, Mendelsohn (1999) argues that sectors that can adjust quickly to climate change can adapt to climate as it unfolds. In this respect, sectors such as agriculture do not generally have long-lasting capital and thus the early depreciation of capital to adjust to climate change would not be necessary. In contrast, the alternative or complementary response strategy encompasses precautionary or planned (ex-ante) adaptations to climate change. In general, planned adaptations are called for through dynamic public policy and are formulated on the basis of robustness, flexibility and net benefits.

Both ex-ante and ex-post adaptation measures can be implemented at numerous levels, including at the global, regional or national level. They can also be incorporated in response strategies adopted by individuals or local communities. In addition, both direct and indirect response strategies aimed to negate concerns about predicted impacts of climate change are included in the possible mix of ex-ante strategies. Such adaptations have been recognized to have the potential to reduce long-term vulnerability as well as realize opportunities associated with climate change, regardless of autonomous adaptation.

It is also important to differentiate between private and public adaptations (Mendelsohn, 1999). Private adaptations are those undertaken only for the exclusive benefit of the individual decision maker. The adoption of various measures will be driven purely by self interest and underlying welfare-maximizing objectives (including profit maximization, output maximization, etc.). In light of high information requirements and/or distribution requirements, or other externalities associated with adaptation, some types of government-sponsored adaptive measures therefore become necessary. While self interest will encourage the adoption of efficient private adaptations, public adaptation will be efficient only with government intervention. The adoption and effectiveness of public adaptations will be thus determined by factors such as the institutional environment, community structure and existing public policy. Mendelsohn (1999) also stresses that joint adaptation needs to be dynamic, particularly in capital-intensive sectors or where there are long-term assets. Policy designs will need to accommodate a series of subtle changes over time as there is unlikely to be one solution that is sufficient to be implemented at any one time.

Adaptation options in agriculture can be categorized loosely within the following framework. First, there are several micro-level adaptation options. These include: farm production adjustments such as diversification and intensification of crop and livestock production; changing land use and irrigation; and altering the timing of operations. Second, there are numerous market responses that have emerged as potentially effective adaptation measures to climate change. Some of the primary measures include development of crop and flood insurance schemes, innovative investment opportunities in crop shares and futures, credit schemes and income diversification opportunities. A third subset of adaptation options encompasses institutional changes that require government responses. These comprise: pricing policy, such as the removal of perverse subsidies; development of income stabilization options; agriculture policy, including agriculture support and insurance programmes; improvement in agriculture markets; and broader goals, such as the promotion of inter-regional trade in agriculture. A fourth (and final) set of adaptation options considered is technological developments. These consist of the development and promotion of new crop varieties and hybrids, advances in water management techniques (e.g. irrigation, conservation tillage), and others.

Observed adaptations to climate change impacts in Africa

In poorer developing countries with weaker financial institutions, particularly in rural areas, there has been more reliance on informal risk-coping strategies. Udry (1990) investigates households in northern Nigeria that simultaneously participate on both sides of the credit market. However, evidence also shows that such strategies are bound by numerous complications that compromise their potential effectiveness. For example, Bardhan and Udry (1999) assert that risk-pooling strategies function well given that information asymmetries are minimized (e.g. due to the limited size of the communities) and the existence of enforcement mechanisms.

Insurance

Recent developments in financial instruments could make climate related insurance in developing countries more favourable than traditional crop insurance programmes, but also make insurance affordable and accessible. The introduction of tradable financial assets such as catastrophic bonds, insurance contracts and other weather markets are examples of recent innovations. The principles of crop insurance programmes are provided in World Bank (2005). Skees et al (2002) highlight the recent effort that was commenced by the International Finance Corporation (IFC) of the World Bank in helping several countries, including Ethiopia, Morocco, Nicaragua and Tunisia, gain access to weather markets as an example of the growing interest in the private provision of weather insurance. Hess and Syroka (2005) explain the development and implementation of a weather-based insurance in southern Africa, with focus on Malawi.

Crop and livestock diversification

Changing farm production practices is one of the most direct methods of adaptation. Diversification of crop and livestock varieties including the replacement of plant types, cultivars, hybrids and animal breeds with new varieties intended for higher drought or heat tolerance have been advocated as having the potential to increase productivity in the face of temperature and moisture stresses.

Diversity in seed genetic structure and composition has been recognized as an effective defence against disease, pest and climate hazards. In a study by Mortimore and Adams (2000), farmers used 3–12 types of pearl millet, 6–22 varieties of sorghum and 14–42 of other cultivars. Seed inventories were from multiple sources including inheritances, own selections from planted material and imported types with recognized advantages over indigenous ones for the new climate. According to the authors, direct transfers of seeds from extension agents were rare although some were traced to agriculture stations within Nigeria or neighbouring Niger. The primary mode of transfer appears to have been outcrossing – where farmers select from types grown in neighbouring farms or even in the wild, and store the seeds for planting in following years. Evidence from the selection of millet seeds, for example, indicates that farmers manage their own genetic pool by selecting and storing the best seeds from each year's crop.

However, numerous constraints can make even this most initial basic adaptation measure difficult. Changing crop location depends on a number of constraints such as the extent of resources and mobility of the affected person(s) and on the availability and conditions (e.g. soil structure and other environmental conditions) in potential destination (land) areas. Switching crop varieties can be expensive because it requires the farmer to possess sufficient knowledge, and support of extension to grow and cultivate crops with which they are less familiar. Moreover, land use regulations or regulations on agriculture production can hinder adaptation of this type. Rigid agriculture and economic programmes, with subsidies for certain crops in certain areas, can constrain change and reduce the flexibility of land use changes. Similarly, farm programmes regulating or subsidizing livestock production systems need to promote flexible adaptation to changed climate.

Changes in intensity and sequencing of production

Altering the intensity of fertilizer and pesticide application as well as capital and labour inputs can help reduce climate change risks to farm production. Changing land use practices such as the location of crop and livestock production, rotating or shifting production between crops and livestock, and shifting production away from marginal areas can help reduce soil erosion and improve moisture and nutrient retention. This includes not only changes in land allocation for different uses, but also the abandonment of land and/or the cultivation of new land, as was shown by El-Shaer et al (1996).

Adjusting the cropping sequence, including changing the timing of sowing, planting, spraying and harvesting to take advantage of the changing duration of growing seasons and associated heat and moisture levels, is another option. Changing the time at which fields are sowed or planted can alter the length of the growing season to better suit the changed environment. Farmer adaptation can also involve changing the timing of irrigation. In a study on Tanzania, O'Brien et al (2000) report that farmers undertake several of such adaptation measures in response to information from climate forecasts.

Improved nutrient and pest control management

Increased CO_2 levels and higher temperatures are likely to induce the need for increased plant protection given the likelihood of increased pest and disease outbreaks. For example, it has been emphasized that this is one reason why pearl millet is a primary crop in the Sahel, a region where poor soils, variation in rainfall and high evapotranspiration make other grains too risky to produce (Fafchamps, 1999). FAO (2000) reports that farmers diversify output through mixed farming systems of crops and livestock as a means of spreading the risk of infrequent, and uncertain, pest and disease infestation.

Temporary migration

It is not clear from the literature to what extent climate change per se can be attributed as the primary factor in the decision-making process of households engaged in agriculture on whether or not to migrate. Tyson et al (2002) find a significant relationship between climate patterns in equatorial Africa and subtropical southern Africa and the southward migration and settlement patterns of the Sotho-Tswana-speaking people from equatorial east Africa. The authors find that changes in rainfall in the two regions influenced migratory patterns. It is accepted that the movement of labour from agriculture into more productive areas and sectors as well as migration between and within urban and rural areas due to environmental, economic or demographic reasons is central to a household's risk-diversification strategy and search for appropriate livelihoods (De Haan, 1999). Migration offers the potential to enhance household ability to withstand shocks and stresses through new or alternative opportunities. Desanker (2002) draws attention to nomadic societies that migrate in response to annual and seasonal rainfall variations in the semi-arid areas such as the Sahel and the Kalahari. It is suggested that the nomadic pastoral systems are intrinsically able to adapt to fluctuating and extreme climates – provided they have sufficient scope for movement, and other necessary elements in the system remain in place.

Adjustments to crop mix

Assuming that there is sufficient knowledge of the changing/changed climatic conditions, and the ability to decide and implement alternative strategies (which in turn will depend on the tenurial arrangement, incomes, etc.), farmers can potentially change crop types. Potential options include switching to more robust varieties that are more appropriate to the new environment, including a more variable climate. For instance, Matarira and Mwamuka (1996) highlight that in Zimbabwe farmers have switched successfully to the use of more drought tolerant crops in areas where the recurrence of droughts has made agriculture production difficult using the traditional crop varieties. In the extreme case, where agriculture is no longer viable, farmers have converted land use from crop production to game ranching. Jolly et al (1995) find that agriculture production in Senegal must be better planned in order to avoid shortages in production below subsistence levels from climate change impacts. In particular, it is recommended that farmers need to adapt by shifting from a cash crop system to a more stable system (e.g. maize), requiring long-term investments in irrigation.

Development of new technologies and modernization

Research and technological innovation in crop and animal productivity have enabled farmers to cope with various climatic conditions and have been fundamental to the growth and development of agriculture. However, in places such as Africa, there is concern that poorer technologies and insufficient agriculture innovation strategies, compounded by other resource and institutional constraints, have contributed to worsening vulnerability to climate variability. In such places there is a need for the continuation and increased support of research on technological options for agriculture development, in addition to the need for correcting institutional shortcomings.

Investment and accumulation of capital

One of the main impediments to adjustment to climate change is poverty itself, whereby lack of resources constrains the ability of farmers to make the necessary adaptations. In a study on Tanzania, O'Brien et al (2000) report that despite numerous adaptation options that farmers are aware of, and willing to apply, the lack of sufficient financial resources and shortage of farmland were among the significant constraints to adaptation. In a similar study on the effect of climate forecasts in Namibia, O'Brien et al (2000) find that serious structural or economic constraints are among the primary reasons for lack of farmer response to the anticipated climate impacts.

Diversification of income earning

Seasonal effects and climatic uncertainty that characterizes the agriculture sector effectively means that diversification of income and employment opportunities is an important adaptation strategy for households in the sector. For example, in Kenya, effective smallholder response to drought has been to shift from traditional planting strategies to employment diversification (Downing et al, 1997).

Note

1. In the 11 countries participating in this study, for 2003, average share of agricultural GDP in country GDP and average share of employment in agriculture were 28 per cent and 67 per cent, respectively. Values of these variables ranged between 4–54 per cent and 30–90 per cent, respectively.

Annex 2: The Household Questionnaire[1]

Manual for Farm Household Survey Questionnaire: Notes to Country Teams and Interviewers

This manual supports the farm household questionnaire that has been designed to obtain data to undertake the Ricardian analysis of climate change impacts on agriculture in Africa. The questionnaire attempts to capture information on pertinent variables that would be utilized to calculate net farm revenue as well as explain the variation in net farm revenue, land values and income across several districts, agroclimatic regions and countries in Africa. This manual outlines various tasks that team leaders of each country in the study need to undertake both prior to and after the completion of interviews as well as instructions and clarifications for the interviewer.

Section I General notes

1. The time period for the survey is the most recent 12-month farming season. Wherever the phrase 'last 12 months' is stated in the survey, this refers to the **most recent** 12-month farming season.
2. Data collection should be based on the survey of predominant **farm types** in districts where agriculture is a major activity. The sample selected for the survey should therefore include households and commercial farms engaged in agriculture during the last 12 months. The farm entities should have cultivated land belonging to its member(s) (i.e. own-farm), to someone else (e.g. rented/sharecropped land (i.e. off-farm), during the last 12 months (see below for details on sampling).
3. Note that for some questions, respondents may provide multiple responses. Please record all such responses.
4. If respondents are unable to provide responses in the specified units, please denote responses in their preferred units and convert to the specified units immediately after completion of the interview.
5. If necessary, please use additional spaces for responses (e.g. on the back of the page on which the question is referred to) with clear reference to the question numbers. These can be incorporated during coding of the data.

Section II Tasks to be completed prior to surveying

The following tasks should be completed by the *country teams* before the interviews are carried out:

1 For the French speaking countries, please translate the questionnaire into French with guidance and assistance from CEEPA.

2 Sampling:

The box below highlights the main conclusions reached during the first meeting of the country teams in Capetown in December 2002. The full report (from which the following content is drawn) can be accessed at http://www.ceepa.co.za/Climate_Change/events.html.

Design of the survey and data collection activities

The following survey design was proposed to guide country-level data collection efforts:

1 The number of data collection units such as districts (DS) is to be within the range of 30–60. This will require some aggregation or disaggregation of available boundaries of survey units. In countries where the number of DS is less than 30, all the DS must be included in the sample.

2 Aggregation/disaggregation of sampling units should be guided by a gradient of climate attributes (i.e. significant change in temperature).

3 Within each survey unit (a DS for example), a minimum of two farm types (FT) (i.e. large and small) and a maximum of five FT (allowing for other farming characteristics of relevance to climate change impact analysis such as cropping system, etc.) are to be surveyed.

4 The survey of farming entities within each FT should target typical farm households in the selected category. It is proposed that a sample within the range of 5–10 households (HH) for each farm type is to be surveyed.

5 The sample size should have a trade-off between the number of HH and the number of DS, keeping in mind each county must spend between $20,000 and $25,000 on this activity.

6 A budget of US$25 per questionnaire was suggested. This means a sample size for each country in the range of 800 and 1000.

7 For example, if a country has 30 DS given three FT it will require a sampling of 10 HH per district for a total sample size of 900.

8 Another example, if a country has 60 DS given three FT it will require a sampling of 5 HH per district for a total sample size of 900.

9 Country teams to advise on budget suggestions.

Each country team should select the primary administrative regions involved in agriculture production to sample based on maps sent by Yale. The sample should be based on the *2nd level administrative regions* in each country. Country teams should sample from those districts that are regarded as a major agricultural district. **The sample selected should be based on the distribution of small, medium and large farms engaged in agriculture and cover the agroclimatic gradient in the country.** These may include farm operations that are for: (a) subsistence only; (b) subsistence and commercial purposes; or (c) purely commercial purposes. **Please send CEEPA a list of the districts to be sampled prior to undertaking the surveys.** This information is also necessary for a number of reasons, including, to enable the International Water Management Institute (IWMI) (South Africa) to estimate and provide runoff and other essential data by districts for the Ricardian analysis.

3 It is recommended that the country team leaders carefully study the questionnaire, convene a meeting with the team of interviewers and provide explanations for questions in the survey. Interviewers should also familiarize themselves with the content of this manual.

4 It is recommended that as much as possible country teams work with extension workers who are likely to be familiar to farmers in their countries. Experience from the pretest suggests that the implementation of the survey will be made easier by working with such groups.

Section III Tasks for team leaders prior to implementing surveys

1 Page 1 of questionnaire: Please ensure that the name of the country and institution that will implement the survey is filled out on the first page.

2 The district code and the assigned household unique ID should be clearly written **on each page of the survey** prior to commencing the interviews.

3 Page 2 of questionnaire: Q1.0.1. Please provide information to the interviewers on the classification of farm size in your respective countries. This information should have been used as the basis for sample selection.

4 Page 3 of questionnaire: Please create a reference key with all local units of measurement of land areas and the corresponding equivalent in hectares (ha) and provide this information to interviewers. The interviewer will require this information prior to commencing an interview in the event that a respondent uses measurement units that are different from those specified in the survey. Interviewers can then use this reference key to convert

measurement units provided by respondents to those specified in the survey after completing each interview.

5   Page 4 of questionnaire: Q3.7.1–Q3.7.3: Please insert the approximate start and end dates of agriculture seasons in your country. For example, this could take the form of Season 1: Start-week1/Apr; End-week3/Jul. An approximation of the start and end dates is acceptable.

6   Page 12 of questionnaire: The questions on income will be utilized as one (among many) indicators of household wellbeing. Given the general sensitivity of this question, interviewers should be careful when obtaining it. If respondents are unwilling to reveal their household income, it is suggested that each country utilize a brief table with possible ranges of income (based on per capita national income distributions in the districts) that respondents can choose from.

An example (NB: please adjust to appropriate range and use local currency):

KEY: $0–<$100 per month
$100–<$300 per month
$300–<$600 per month
$600–<$1000
More than $1000 per month

7   Page 12 of questionnaire: Q6.3: If respondent is unwilling to provide this information, country team leaders should use government-published tax rates and estimate the amount paid in taxes for 6.3.1–6.3.4 based on responses to 6.1 and 6.2.

8   Page 14 of questionnaire: Team leaders: please assign a unique ID for each respondent in the survey. The ID should be a unique number within the sample size for each district. It is suggested that the ID ranges from 1 to n where n is the total number of farms sampled in a particular district.

Section IV Instructions to interviewer

Page 1 of questionnaire

1   The survey respondent should ideally be the head of the farm entity. However, as the head may not always be available during field visits, the next most senior adult household member should be interviewed. In the case of a large-scale farm (commercial entity), the respondent should be the owner of the farm entity. If the owner is not available, the manager or foreman of the farm should be interviewed.

2 Please read the introductory paragraph to the interviewee of the farm entity when contacting to interview. Emphasize that responses will be confidential.

3 If respondent is willing to complete the interview, please record the current time and commence survey.

Page 2 of questionnaire

The information requested on household composition will be used with other socio-economic variables to explain the variation in productivity and farm revenue across farm households.

1.0.1 Please record the type of farm household being interviewed. This should be inferred from the country's sample design. Team leaders should provide an appropriate scale as specified in Section II(8) of this manual.

1.0.2 Record the relationship of interviewee to the head of the household. The Family member code (FMC) will be as follows: 1 Head of household/ owner of commercial farm; 2 Husband; 3 Wife; 4 Child; 5 Grandchild; 6 Parent of head of household; 7 Sibling of head of household; 8 Other family member (includes household helpers); 9 Manager of farm operations.

NB: If the manager of a farm is responding to the questions, please ensure that the information in Section 1 of the survey refers to the household of the **owner of the farm**. This information should be obtained directly from the owner or with the best of the knowledge of the manager.

1.1 and 1.2 Include the total number of only household members who have been residing (including consuming meals and sleeping) in the household for at least the last 12 months (including infants under 1 year). In the case of commercial farms, household members refer to the family members of the owner.

1.2.1–1.2.6 It is recommended that you start with the household head, then the male or female members of the household.

1.2.1 Code for gender: 1 Male; 2 Female.

1.2.2 Age as of 30 June 2003.

1.2.3 Marital status: Please use the key provided to denote responses. Married couples include those who have formally entered into marriage, or are living together under other traditional arrangement. Other options include previously married but currently divorced, separated, widowed.

1.2.4 Education should be recorded in terms of formal schooling years completed. Additional year(s) spent repeating a school year due to failure to complete for any reason should not be counted. If household member has not been to school denote with zero (0).

1.2.5 An individual is deemed to be working on farm activities, if he/she is engaged in any (physical or non-physical) activity that contributes directly or indirectly to the production of output from the household owned or any other farm.

1.2.6 Non-farm activities include any non-agriculture activities that a household member may be involved in either full- or part-time.

Use additional space on the back of the page if household size is greater than 8. Please remember to number the questions and corresponding responses correctly.

1.4 Please use the following key:
   KEY for 1.4: 1 Nonreligious;   3 Islam;
                       2 Christian;   4 African Traditional Religion;
                       5 Other (pls. specify_____).

1.5 If the household is connected to the national power grid, denote '1'. If the household is NOT connected to the national grid (i.e. has any other source of energy – such as own generator, solar, biogas, etc.), denote '2'.

Page 3 of questionnaire

2.1–2.2 The following classification is an example of possible responses:

1 Farmer	7 Health worker
2 Agriculture (farm) labourer	8 Trader
3 Artisan	9 Student
4 Office worker	10 Unemployed
5 Civil servant	11 Not in labour force
6 Teacher	12 Other non-agriculture worker

2.3 and 2.5 We are interested in obtaining the average number of days (per week) spent on primary and secondary occupations. By definition, **1 day of work = 6–8 hours of work (NB: The total number of days spent per week on primary and secondary occupation must be = 7).**

2.7 We are interested in a measure of the number of days a person was incapacitated from undertaking any work (both primary and secondary occupations).

Pages 3–4 of questionnaire

PLEASE NOTE THAT THE **QUESTIONS IN SECTION 3 ARE EXTREMELY IMPORTANT FOR ESTIMATING NET REVENUE.**

NB: Interviewer: Please ensure that the denoted units of the quantity of land in Q3.1a and Q3.1c is converted to the equivalent of hectares (ha) upon completion of the interview.

3.1a and 3.1.1 Definition of PLOT:

A For small-scale and medium-scale farms

1   If the total farmland is effectively a **single** block of land area (irrespective of its size – i.e. respondent chose option 1 to question 3.1), then treat the total farmland as 1 PLOT.
2   If the total farmland is **divided into several blocks** (i.e. respondent chose option 2, 3 or 4 in question 3.1) **but the total area of farm land = 5ha (approximately)**, the farmland is effectively 1 PLOT.
3   If the total farmland is **divided into several blocks,** and the total area is (approximately) > 5ha then treat the **largest area** (as denoted in 3.1a.1) as PLOT 1 and the sum of ALL other areas (3.1a.2 and 3.1a.3) as PLOT 2.

This in effect means the majority of small-scale farms surveyed will have 1 plot, and a few cases will have 2 plots.

Example A:
3.1 *how many separated land areas are used as farmland?*
3.1a *Please ask about the size of 2 largest fields:*
3.1a.1   Largest single area: 5
3.1a.2   2nd largest single area: 2
3.1a.3   Cumulative size of all remaining areas: 1.5

So, according to the definition in **(A)**, this farm has **2 PLOTS** and
        Total Area of PLOT1 = 5 (equals amount in 3.1a.1)
        Total Area of PLOT2 = 3.5 (equals sum of amount in 3.1a.2 and 3.1a.3)

NB: If units are in something other than hectares (ha), then interviewer will need to convert to ha. **COUNTRY TEAM LEADERS**: Please create a key with all local units of measurement of land areas and the corresponding equivalent in ha and provide this information to interviewers. They will require this data prior to commencing an interview.

B For large-scale (commercial) farms

1   If the total farmland is effectively **a single block** of land area (irrespective of its size – i.e. respondent chose option 1 to question 3.1), then treat the total farmland as 1 PLOT.
2   If the total farmland is **divided into several blocks**, (i.e. respondent chose option 2, 3 or 4 in question 3.1) **but the total area of farm land = 20ha (approximately)**, the farmland is effectively 1 PLOT.
3   If the total farmland is **divided into several blocks**, but the total area is (approximately) > 20ha then treat the **largest area** (as denoted in 3.1a.1) as PLOT 1 and the sum of ALL other areas (3.1a.2 and 3.1a.3) as PLOT 2.

Example B:

3.1 *How many separate areas are used as farmland?* 4

3.1a *Please ask about the size of 3 largest fields:*

3.1a.1   Largest single area: 40

3.1a.2   2nd largest single area: 35

3.1a.3   Cumulative size of all remaining areas: 35

So, this large-scale (commercial) farm with *a cumulative area* of 110ha of farmland (with separate land areas farmed), has effectively **2 plots.**

Total area of PLOT1 = 40 (equals amount in 3.1a.1)

Total area of PLOT2 = 70 (equals sum of amount in 3.1a.2 and 3.1a.3)

NB: Interviewer: If units are in something other than ha, then interviewer will need to convert to ha.

COUNTRY TEAM LEADERS: Please create a key with all local units of measurement of land areas and the corresponding equivalent in ha and provide this information to interviewers. They will require these data prior to commencing an interview.

Page 4 of questionnaire

3.2   The following classification is an example of possible responses for system of farming. Please allow for others that may not be in this list. (**Interviewer:** *please allow for multiple responses.*)

  1 Shifting cultivation (with long fallow period);
  2 Continuous cropping (no fallow period);
  3 Continuous cropping with multiple rotations (includes short fallow period);
  4 Livestock grazing land;
  5 Other (pls. specify ...).

3.3   The following classification is an example of possible responses for type of tenure. (**Interviewer:** *Please allow for multiple responses.*)

  1 Own land and own use;   5 Rented land;
  2 Own land and rent to others;   6 Borrowed land (do not pay for
  3 Sharecropped land;   usage);
  4 Communal land;   7 Other (pls. specify...).

3.4   For PLOT 1 (i.e. largest unit of farm land), please ask number of years the plot has been in operation. In the case of Plot 2, please provide an average estimate of the number of years that all other farmland has been in operated. If respondent is unable to provide an average estimate of the number of years that all other areas (i.e. PLOT 2) has been in operation, please denote either the number of years that each of the remaining areas have been used as farmland, or the year that each of the separate areas commence operation. Convert these years into an average immediately after the interview.

NB: Interviewer: If the respondent has been farming lands that have been passed to him by family (e.g. heritage) please note the response and code it appropriately. Contact CEEPA or Yale for guidance.

3.6 The purpose of this question is to elicit an approximate value/worth of the farm operations (including value of land, buildings, equipment, animals). If interviewee traditionally inherits or passes land within family/community, please ask question 3.6.1.

3.7.1–3.7.3 Country teams should have inserted the start month and end month of seasons in each country. An approximate estimate is sufficient.

Page 5 of questionnaire

3.8 Workers include household members as well as hired (full-time/part-time) labour. Adults are defined as any individual of 16 years of age or older. Children are defined as individuals less than 16 years of age.

3.8.2.1–3.8.2.3 and 3.8.3.1–3.8.3.3 and 3.8.4.

For each type of farm activity, please denote the total number of household and hired labour as well as the average number of days worked by the various categories of labour.

The number of workers ('No') column should record the total number of workers of the specified category. The 'Days' column should record *the average number of days* worked by **1 individual**. By definition, **1 day = 6–8 hours** of work completed by 1 individual.

Page 6 of questionnaire

3.9.1 (a–c) Please denote the average wage/day per class of family member.

3.9.1 (e–g) Please denote the average wage/day per class of hired member.

3.9.2 (a–c) Please denote total in-kind payments/day for each type of family member.

3.9.2 (e–g) Please denote in-kind payments/day for each type of hired member.

Pages 6–7 of questionnaire

PLEASE NOTE THAT THE **QUESTIONS IN SECTION 4 ARE EXTREMELY IMPORTANT FOR ESTIMATING NET REVENUE.**

4.1 Please use the following key for crops.

1 alfalfa	15 cucumber	29 okra	43 sheanut
2 banana	16 enset	30 onion	44 sorghum
3 barley	17 field pea	31 palm dates	45 soybean

4 beans	18 flax	32 paprika	46 spinach
5 cashew	19 garden-eggs	33 peanuts	47 squash
6 cassava	20 garlic	34 pepper	48 sugar cane
7 chickpeas	21 grape	35 pigeon pea	49 sunflower
8 citrus fruits	22 groundnut	36 pineapple	50 tea
9 clover	23 kola	37 plantain	51 tef
10 cocoa	24 lentil	38 potato	52 tobacco
11 cocoyam	25 mango	39 rice	53 tomato
12 cowpea	26 maize	40 safflower	54 wheat
13 coffee	27 millet	41 sesame	55 yam
14 cotton	28 oil palm	42 shallots	56 other (specify)

If there are crops which are not included in the list, classify them under '56 Other'.

4.1.1 Please refer to definition of plot on pages 3–4 of this questionnaire.

4.1.2 Please refer to crop codes provided under 4.1.

4.2–4.3 Please provide the approximate dates of planting and harvesting. We require an approximate period during which these activities commence. Please be as specific as possible (e.g. 1st week of April, etc.).

4.4   Record the proportion of **plot area** cultivated by each crop.

NB: Interviewer: For the following questions (4.5–4.9 and 4.11) respondents can provide their responses in any other appropriate unit. Please convert to the specified unit after completion of the interview.

4.5   This includes all harvests over the specified season.

4.6–4.7 Enter amount of harvest that is consumed by the household and livestock. If the crop that is consumed is from the 2 specified plots, then estimate the average for a single plot. This amount also includes the amount kept as storage for household consumption.

4.8   Enter amount of crop harvest losses due to disease and pests outbreaks in each season.

4.9   Enter amount (in kg) of harvest that is sold in the market place. If the amount is specified in another unit, record that unit and convert to kg AFTER completion of the interview.

4.9a   Please note to whom the output is sold:
       KEY for 4.9a: 1 directly to consumers by farm entity; 2 middleman/wholesale establishment who in turn sells output to consumers; 3 other.

4.10   Please ensure that *farm-gate* value is recorded. This is the value based on what the farmer directly receives from the sale of his output and NOT the market price.

4.11a If farmer is unable to provide an estimate of the amount of seeds used in kg, then note the units in which he is able to provide a response (# bags, etc) and convert to kg using a suitable conversion factor. Please ensure the conversion factor is recorded and reported in the final data sets.

4.11b This is based on the market price of seeds.

Page 8 of questionnaire

4.12.0 Please only note codes of 5 principal crops (i.e. in terms of value). Please use crop codes provided for Q4.1 and Q4.1.2.

4.12.1 'Normal year average yield' refers to the average yield in a year where there are no unusual (e.g. drought, etc.) weather effects. The normal year can be selected over the previous 5–10 years. The measurement should be in terms of kg/ha. If alternative units are used, record units and convert to kg/ha on completion of the interview.

4.13.2 Please allow for multiple responses to water sources to farm. The following are examples of likely responses although it is recommended that the interviewer allows for others:

KEY for 4.13.2: 1 Irrigated major scheme (public);
2 Irrigated minor scheme (private);
3 Irrigated – groundwater;
4 Rainfed;
5 Other (pls. specify...).

4.13.3 Please note that respondents should be allowed to provide more than one option as an answer:

KEY for 4.13.3: 1 Gravity;
2 Sprinklers;
3 Drip systems;
4 Other (please specify in space provided in the column).

4.13.4–4.13.5 Please record the amount (kg) of fertilizer and pesticide used in each plot per year.

4.14–4.15 Please record the average cost per kg of inputs (fertilizer and pesticide). If farmers are unable to answer, country teams should denote average price for the district concerned.

NB: Interviewers: 4.13.4–4.15 If the unit of measurement is an alternative, please convert to kg at the most convenient time immediately AFTER the completion of the interview.

Page 9 of questionnaire

NB: Interviewer: In Section 4.16, wherever it states *'Other pls. specify...'* use additional space to record each item and information requested in 4.16.1–4.16.3a.

4.16.1   Record the number of each type of primary machinery used in farm activities over the last 12 months.

4.16.2   Machinery can be owned by the farm entity, jointly owned with other households or rented. Please record which of the following options applies for each item of machinery:

KEY for 4.16.2: 1 Household/commercial farm has ownership;
                 2 Jointly owned with other households/farm entities;
                 3 Hired for household or joint use.

4.16.3   If a tool, machinery, or implement is privately owned by a member of the farm entity, denote the purchase price/unit. If machinery is hired, record the total fee/unit paid. If jointly owned, enter the amount contributed to the purchase of the jointly owned item.

NB: Team leaders: If respondent has difficulty answering these questions, country team should estimate value of equipment based on current market price in the districts concerned.

4.16.3a Please provide information on the average lifespan on the machinery.

NB: Country teams can estimate lifespan based on information from other local sources (such as extension agents).

4.16.4   Please only include buildings owned by the farming entity. Buildings are defined as permanent construction structures that are used specifically for farm activities.

Please provide an approximate value of the buildings and indication of their purpose.

KEY for 4.16.6: 1 Space for storage of agriculture products;
                 2 Space for farm activities (crop and livestock activities);
                 3 Space for housing of agriculture workers;
                 4 Space for storage of farm equipment;
                 5 Other uses.

NB: Interviewer: If responses to the value of the building are difficult, please inquire about how much it would cost to purchase a similar building.

Page 10 of questionnaire

4.17.1–4.17.3 Distance can be measured in terms of average km or hours. Preference is to measure in terms of distance. Please specify which unit is used.

KEY for 4.17.2: 1 Walk;
                 2 Animal;
                 3 Cart;
                 4 Truck or other motorized vehicle;
                 5 Other (pls. specify).

4.18   If response is no this question, skip following questions and go directly to question 4.20.

4.18.1 and 4.19.1 Wherever it states *'Other pls. specify...'* use additional space to record each item and corresponding information requested. If game farming is practised on the farm, please classify this as also part of *'Other pls. specify...'* and denote answers to corresponding questions.

4.18.2 Please denote approximate number of animals owned by farm entity at the commencement of the agriculture year (i.e. on 1st day of 1st month of the last 12-month period).

4.18.3.1 Include number of animals lost through theft, diseases, prey animals, etc. for the year.

4.19.1 Milk products include cheeses, yogurts, etc.

4.19.2 and 4.19.4 **NB: Interviewer:** If responses are in a different unit to kg, please note the new unit during the interview and then convert to kg/year after the completion of the survey using an appropriate scale. Please highlight the scale on the survey next to the table.

Page 11 of questionnaire

4.20 Please record the TOTAL COST per year for each of the row items.

4.20.1.3 and 4.20.2.3: STORAGE COSTS: Storage costs include cost of maintaining agriculture produce (e.g. cost of granary, refrigeration, etc.). This includes the physical as well as other storage related costs (e.g. spraying, etc.).

Section 5 is on extension services. Extension is defined as including any assistance (in the form of advice, training or information) that farmers receive from an external agent(s) (i.e. not member of household).

5.3 This question is meant to understand whether farmers obtain advice on crop and livestock production from other sources apart from assistance from official extension agents. This question asks about informal sources of extension advice.

KEY for 5.3:1 Media;

2 Neighbouring farmer;

3 Shopkeepers in village;

4 Others (pls. specify...);

5 None.

The option '5 none' means the farmer receives extension information and advice from only formal extension agents.

Page 12 of questionnaire

NB: Country teams The questions on income will be utilized as one (among many) indicator of household wellbeing. Given the general sensitivity of this question, interviewers should be careful when obtaining it. If respondents are unwilling to reveal their actual household income, it is suggested that the interviewer utilize a brief table with possible ranges of income (based on per capita national income distributions in the districts that respondents can choose from).

An example: (NB: please adjust to appropriate range and use local currency):

KEY: 1 $0–<$100 per month

2 $100–<$300 per month

3 $300–<$600 per month

4 $600–<$1000

5 More than $1000 per month

NB: COUNTRY TEAM LEADERS – Please provide this table to the interviewer

For questions 6.1–6.2.1, **net** income means income AFTER the amount paid as income tax has been deducted. 'normal average year' refers to a year where there are no unusual (e.g. drought, etc.) weather effects. The normal year can be selected over the previous 5–10 years.

6.1 and 6.2 Please note that total NET household income includes income from both farm (own farm and off-farm (e.g. if household member works on someone else's farm)) and non-farm activities.

6.1.1 and 6.2.1 These focus on income from non-farm/non-agriculture sources such as salaries, gifts, pensions and other government support.

6.5.2 Examples of sources of agriculture subsidies include:

KEY: 1 From the government;

2 From non-governmental organization (NGO);

3 From private sector sources;

4 From other (pls. specify source).

Page 13 of questionnaire

7.0   We would like to know for how long the respondent has been practising farming (in number of years). If respondent has been a farmer all his life, please indicate current age.

In Section 7, we seek brief but detailed responses on the types of adjustments in farming practices, such as changing crops, acres planted, planting and harvest dates, that farmers are currently undertaking because of rainfall and temperature changes.

Section V Tasks to be completed AFTER survey is completed

Page 13: **Interviewer:** Please complete this page upon completion of the interview. It is extremely important in order to clarify unusual observations among others reasons (e.g. permit mapping of findings of the survey).

It is highly recommended that contact information for the respondent is also recorded on this page in order to help with any future follow up activities.

Page 9: Q4.16.3a: Country teams should estimate the lifespan of machinery based on information from other local sources (such as extension agents). If respondent has failed to answer this question district averages can then be utilized.

Note

1. Based on questionnaire prepared by School of Forestry and Environmental Sciences, Yale University (USA) and Centre for Environmental Economics and Policy in Africa (CEEPA), University of Pretoria, South Africa.

Questionnaire on Farm Households

Introductory statement:

'Scientific evidence has confirmed that the climate will likely change in the future with implications for agriculture. The information provided by you in this interview about your farm activities in the last 12 months' farming season will contribute to understanding the likely impacts of climate on agriculture in _____ [country team: *Insert name of country*] and in Africa as a whole. Your responses to these questions will be anonymous.

Time interview began: _____

District Code: _____; Household ID: _____

Page 2

This country study is being conducted by _____
(Country team: *Please write the name of your institution in the space provided.*)

Thank you for your kind cooperation.'

1.0.1 Type of farm entity:
KEY for 1.0.1: 1 Small-scale; 2 Medium scale; 3 Large-scale (Interviewer: *Please complete this question following the classification of farm types in the country's sample design.*)
1.0.2 Please state the relationship of the respondent to the head of the household of the farm: _____
KEY for 1.0.2: 1 Head of household; 2 Husband; 3 life; 4 Child; 5 Grandchild; 6 Parents; 7 Siblings; 8 Other family members (includes household helpers); 9 Manager/other proxy for owner.

Section 1: Household roster – Members of households and education

1.1 Household size (of owner of the farm):
1.2 Household characteristics.

	1.2.1	1.2.2	1.2.3	1.2.4	1.2.5	1.2.6
	Gender	Age	Marital status	Education (in number of years)	Work on farm activities?	Work on non-farm activities?
1						
2						
3						
4						
5						
6						
7						
8						
	KEY for 1.2.1: 1 Male 2 Female		**KEY for 1.2.3:** 1 Married or living together under local custom 2 Never married 3 Previously married (currently divorced, separated, widowed). 4 Not applicable (child < 16 years)		**KEY for 1.2.5:** 1 yes 2 no	**KEY for 1.2.6:** 1 yes 2 no

District Code: _____; Household ID: _____

Please use additional space on back of page if necessary.

1.3 Which tribe does the household head belong to? _____

1.4 What religion does the head of the household practise? _____

KEY for 1.4: 1 Nonreligious; 2 Christianity; 3 Islam; 4 African Traditional Religion; 5 Other (pls. specify …).

1.5 Does the household have electricity? _____

KEY for 1.5: 1 yes; 2 no.

Section 2: Employment – All questions pertain to the last 12 months

2.1	2.2	2.3	2.4	2.5	2.6	2.7
What is the primary occupation of the head of the household?	What is the secondary occupation of the head of the household?	Number of **days** (per week) spent on primary occupation	Number of **weeks** over the last 12 months spent on primary occupation	Number of **days** (per week) spent on secondary occupation	Number of **weeks** over the last 12 months spent on secondary occupation	Number of work **days** lost due to illness over the last 12 months
KEY for 2.1 and 2.2: 1 Farmer 2 Agriculture (farm) labourer 3 Artisan 4 Office worker 5 Civil Servant 6 Teacher	7 Health worker 8 Trader 9 Student 10 Unemployed 11 Not in labour force 12 Other non-agriculture worker	*(By definition, 1 day of work = 6–8 hours of work.)*		*(By definition, 1 day of work = 6–8 hours of work.)*		

Section 3: Tenure issues and labour composition – All questions pertain to the last 12 months

3.1 How many **separated** land areas are used as farmland? (Interviewer: If response is '1', respond to 3.1a.1 and 3.1a.4 only)
KEY for 3.1:
1 only 1 single area is farmed;
2 2 separate areas are farmed;
3 3 separate areas are farmed;
4 >3 separate areas are farmed

3.1a Please denote the size of the **following** separated farmed land areas used over the last 12 months: _____ (Interviewer: *Please denote the unit in which the quantity of land is measured locally during interview.*)

3.1a.1 Largest single area: _____ (**NB:** Interviewer: *This area is what is referred to as PLOT 1 in the ensuing questions that make reference to a 'plot'.*)

3.1a.2 2nd largest single area: _____ (**NB:** Interviewer: *This cumulative area is referred to as PLOT 2 in the ensuing questions.*)

3.1a.3 Cumulative size of all remaining areas: _____
Area 3: (Sum ALL remaining areas): _____

3.1a.4 Unit of measurement of land areas in 3.1a.1–3.1a.3: _____
(ha, acres, etc. *Pls. specify*)

District Code: _____; Household ID: _____

Page 4

Please answer the following land use questions with respect to total amount and type of land operated by members of household:

3.1.1	3.2	3.3	3.4	3.5
Plot numbers	System of farming	Tenure type	How many (average) number of years have you used these plots?	Total rent paid (per month) if pilot is leased
1				
2				

KEY for 3.2:
1 Shifting cultivation (with long fallow period);
2 Continuous cropping (no fallow period);
3 Continuous cropping with multiple rotations; (includes short fallow period)
4 Livestock grazing land;
5 Other (pls. specify...).
(**Interviewer:** *Please allow for multiple response*)

KEY for 3.3:
1 Own land and own use;
2 Own land and rent to others;
3 Sharecropped land;
4 Communal land (traditional ownership);
5 Rented land;
6 Borrowed land (do not pay for usage);
7 Other (pls. specify...).
(**Interviewer:** *Please allow for multiple responses*)

3.6. If this farm (including land, buildings, equipment and livestock) were for sale, what is its approximate value? _____

(Interviewer: *If response to above is difficult, go to question 3.6.1. Otherwise, go to 3.7.1.*)

3.6.1 If you were to purchase a farm identical to yours (including land, buildings, equipment and livestock), what would you have to pay for it? _____

3.7.1–3.7.3 TO BE COMPLETED BY TEAM LEADER PRIOR TO COMMENCING INTERVIEWS

KEY for 3.7.1c, 3.7.2c and 3.7.3c

3.7.1 Agriculture season 1:	3.7.1a: Start:	3.7.1b: End:	3.7.1c: Season:
3.7.2 Agriculture season 2:	3.7.2a: Start:	3.7.2b: End:	3.7.2c: Season:
3.7.3 Agriculture season 3:	3.7.3a: Start:	3.7.3b: End:	3.7.3c: Season:

1: winter season; 2: summer season; 3: Other season (pls. specify ...).

District Code: _____; Household ID: _____

3.8 Division of labour information by activity for each season

3.8.2 Total estimated number of farm workers and days worked (per activity for each season) (1 day = 6–8 hours of work completed by 1 individual)

3.8.1 Season and type of activity		Household labour						Hired labour					
		3.8.2.1 Male Adult		3.8.2.2 Adult female		3.8.2.3 Child (<16 years)		3.8.3.1 Male Adult		3.8.3.2 Female Adult		3.8.3.3 Child (<16 years)	
		a No	b Days	a No	b Days	a No	b Days	a No	b Days	a No	b Days	a No	b Days
Season 1	11 Land preparation												
	12 Planting												
	13 Weeding												
	14 Pesticide, fertilizer, irrigation, etc.												
	15 Harvesting												
	16 Post-harvest processing												
	17 Other activities (farm management, maintenance, etc.)												
	21 Land preparation												
	22 Planting												
	23 Weeding												
	24 Pesticide, fertilizer, irrigation, etc.												
	25 Harvesting												

District Code: _____; Household ID: _____

3.8 Division of labour information by activity for each season

3.8.2 Total estimated number of farm workers and days worked (per activity for each season) (Cont'd) (1 day = 6–8 hours of work completed by 1 individual)

3.8.1 Season and type of activity	Household labour						Hired labour					
	3.8.2.1 Adult Male		3.8.2.2 Adult female		3.8.2.3 Child (<16 years)		3.8.3.1 Adult		3.8.3.2 Adult Female		3.8.3.3 Child (<16 years)	
	a No	b Days	a No	b Days	a No	b Days	a No Male	b Days	a No	b Days	a No	b Days
Season 2												
26 Post-harvest processing												
27 Other activities (farm management, maintenance, etc.)												
31 Land preparation												
32 Planting												
33 Weeding												
34 Pesticide, fertilizer, irrigation, etc.												
35 Harvesting												
Season 3												
36 Post-harvest processing												
37 Other activities (farm management, maintenance, etc.)												
3.8.4 Livestock-animal management (*annual estimate*)												

District Code: _____ ; Household ID: _____

3.9	Farm wage rates	Household labour			Hired labour		
		Adult male	Adult female	Child	Adult male	Adult female	Child
3.9.1	Average **wage/day** (across various activities) for each type of worker	3.9.1a	3.9.1b	3.9.1c	3.9.1e	3.9.1f	3.9.1g
3.9.2	Total in-kind payments **per day** (across various activities)	3.9.2a	3.9.2b	3.9.2c	3.9.2e	3.9.2f	3.9.2g

Section 4: Details on farming activities – Part 1: Food and tree crops

All questions pertain to the last 12 months

4.1. Information on the primary crops grown in your farm over the last 12 months.

Please use the following **KEY for 4.1.2**: (If a crop is not listed below, please denote as 'other' and specify.)

1	alfalfa	11	cocoyam	21	grape	31	palm dates	41	sesame	51	tef
2	banana	12	cowpea	22	groundnut	32	paprika	42	shallots	52	tobacco
3	barley	13	coffee	23	kola	33	peanuts	43	sheanut	53	tomato
4	beans	14	cotton	24	lentil	34	pepper	44	sorghum	54	wheat
5	cashew	15	cucumber	25	mango	35	pigeon pea	45	soybean	55	yam
6	cassava	16	enset	26	maize	36	pineapple	46	spinach	56	other
7	citrus fruit	17	field pea	27	millet	37	plantain	47	squash		
8	chickpeas	18	flax	28	oil palm	38	potato	48	sugar cane		
9	clover	19	garden–eggs	29	okra	39	rice	49	sunflower		
10	cocoa	20	garlic	30	onion	40	safflower	50	tea		

District Code: _____ ; Household ID: _____

Please use additional space if there are more than 6 crops per plot.

Season	4.1.1 Plot no.	4.1.2 Crop type (Use key for 4.1.2 above)	4.2 Planting date	4.3 Harvest date	4.4 Proportion of plot area cultivated with crop (%)	4.5 Quantity harvested (kg) (Includes all harvests)	4.6 Amount consumed by household (kg)	4.7 Amount consumed by livestock (kg)	4.8 Amount lost due to disease and pests (kg)	4.9 Quantity sold (kg)	4.9a To whom is output sold?	4.10 Total value of crops sold (Farm-gate value)	4.11a Amount of seeds used (kg)	4.11b Cost/kg of seed
1	1													
	2													
2	1													
	2													

District Code: _____ ; Household ID: _____

Season	4.1.1 Plot no.	4.1.2 Crop type (Use key for 4.1.2 above)	4.2 Planting date	4.3 Harvest date	4.4 Proportion of plot area cultivated with crop (%)	4.5 Quantity harvested (kg) (Includes all harvests)	4.6 Amount consumed by household (kg)	4.7 Amount consumed by livestock (kg)	4.8 Amount lost due to disease and pests (kg)	4.9 Quantity sold (kg)	4.9a To whom is output sold?	4.10 Total value of crops sold (Farm-gate value)	4.11a Amount of seeds used (kg)	4.11b Cost/kg of seed
	1													
	2													
3														
	Interviewer additional	Please use space if necessary									**KEY for 4.9a:** 1 Directly to consumers; 2 Middleman /wholesale; establishment 3 Other.			

District Code: _____ ; Household ID: _____

4.12 Please state the average yield of your 5 principal crops in a *normal* year.

4.12.0 Crop type (use code specified in 4.1) _____

Crop 1
Crop 2
Crop 3
Crop 4
Crop 5

4.12.1 Normal year average yield (in terms of kg/ha) _____

KEY for 4.12.0 (If a crop is not listed below, please denote as 'other' and specify.)

1	alfalfa	11	cocoyam	21	grape	31	palm dates
2	banana	12	cowpea	22	groundnut	32	paprika
3	barley	13	coffee	23	kola	33	peanuts
4	beans	14	cotton	24	lentil	34	pepper
5	cashew	15	cucumber	25	mango	35	pigeon pea
6	cassava	16	enset	26	maize	36	pineapple
7	citrus fruit	17	field pea	27	millet	37	plantain
8	chickpeas	18	flax	28	oil palm	38	potato
9	clover	19	garden-eggs	29	okra	39	rice
10	cocoa	20	garlic	30	onion	40	safflower

41	sesame	51	tef
42	shallots	52	tobacco
43	sheanut	53	tomato
44	sorghum	54	wheat
45	soybean	55	yam
46	spinach	56	other
47	squash		
48	sugar cane		
49	sunflower		
50	tea		

District Code: _____ ; Household ID: _____

Page 10

4.13.0	4.13.1	4.13.2	4.13.3	4.13.4	4.13.5
Season	Plot no.	Water source (Interviewer: Please allow for multiple sources. If response is 4 only, please skip to 4.13.4; otherwise, go to 4.13.3.)	If you use irrigation, which system do you use? (Interviewer: Please allow for multiple responses.)	Fertilizer use (kg/year)	Pesticide use (kg/year)
1	1				
	2				
2	1				
	2				
3	1				
	2				
		KEY for 4.13.2: 1 Irrigated-major scheme (public); 2 Irrigated minor scheme (private); 3 Irrigated – groundwater; 4 Rainfed 5 Other (pls. specify ...).	KEY for 4.13.3: 1 Gravity; 2 Sprinklers; 3 Drip systems; 4 Other (pls. specify ...).		

District Code: _____ ; Household ID: _____

4.14 Cost/kg of fertilizer: _____

4.15 Cost/kg of pesticide: _____

4.16 Information on farm machinery and inputs and farm buildings

Tool/Machinery/Implements	4.16.1 Number	4.16.2 Who owns the equipment?	4.16.3 Price (or value)/unit	4.16.3a Average lifespan of item
Light machinery				
1 Cutlass, machete				
2 Hoe				
3 File				
4 Axe				
5 Baskets				
6 Weeder				
7 Other light machinery (pls. specify ...)				
Heavy machinery				
8 Tractor				
9 Plough				
10 Trolley/Trailers				
11 Thresher				

District Code: _____ ; Household ID: _____

Tool/Machinery/Implements	4.16.1 Number	4.16.2 Who owns the equipment?	4.16.3 Price (or value)/unit	4.16.3a Average lifespan of item
12 Fodder cutting machine				
13 Generator/diesel pumps				
14 Spraying machines (chem./fertilizer)				
15 Other heavy machinery (pls. specify ....)				
Farm animal power				
16 Bullocks				
17 Mules				
18 Other animal power (pls. specify ....)				
NB: for (7), (15) and (18), please specify each item and information requested in 4.16.1–4.16.3a using additional space on back of page.	**KEY for 4.16.2:** 1 Household has ownership; 2 Jointly owned with other households/farm entities; 3 Hired for household or joint use.			

District Code: _____ ; Household ID: _____

4.16.4 Please provide information on the buildings used to support agriculture production activities (table below).

4.16.4a Building no.	4.16.4b Purpose (Interviewer: *Please allow for multiple responses.*)	4.16.4c Value
Building 1		
Building 2		
Building 3		
	KEY for 4.16b: 1 Space for storage of agriculture products; 2 Space for farm activities (crop and livestock activities); 3 Space for housing of agriculture workers; 4 Space for storage of farm equipment; 5 Other uses.	

District Code: _____; Household ID: _____

Page 14

4.17.1 How far is it to the nearest market where you **sell** your harvest? (a) In distance: _____ (km); **or** (b) In time _____ (hrs)

4.17.2 What transport do you use to get to market? _____

KEY for 4.17.2:
1 Walk; 2 Animal; 3 Cart; 4 Truck or other motorized vehicle; 5 Other (specify).

4.17.3 How far is it to the nearest market where you **obtain** your inputs? In distance: (a) _____ (kms); **or** (b) _____ in time (hrs)

Section 4: Details on farming activities – Part 2: Livestock, poultry and other farm animals

4.18 Does your household own livestock, poultry or other farm animals? _____ 1: yes; 0: no
(If no, please continue to Section 4.20)

4.18.1	4.18.2	4.18.3	4.18.3.1	4.18.4	4.18.5	4.18.6			4.18.7	4.18.8
Type	Number Currently owned	Number born over last 12 months	Number of animals lost, stolen, killed by disease/prey, etc. over last 12 months	Number purchased over last 12 months	Purchase price (per animal)	Number of months that animals graze on			Number sold over last 12 months	Sale price (per animal)
						Communal land	Own land	Open land		
1 Cattle (for meat)										
2 Cattle (for milk)										
3 Breeding bulls										
4 Goat										
5 Sheep										
6 Pigs for breeding										
7 Oxen										
8 Chicken										
9 Other (specify …)										

District Code: _____ ; Household ID: _____

4.19.1 Own livestock products	4.19.2 Quantity for own use (kg/year)	4.19.3 Quantity sold (kg/year)	4.19.4 Price per unit
1 Milk products			
Meat (slaughtering)			
2 Beef			
3 Sheep			
4 Goat			
5 Other (specify)			
Other products			
6 Eggs			
7 Wool			
8 Leather			
9 Other (pls. specify ....)			

District Code: _____ ; Household ID: _____

Page 16

4.20 Can you please tell us the total cost of the following activities?

Code	Type	4.20.1 Food and tree crops harvested	4.20.2 Livestock
1	Transport costs	4.20.1.1	4.20.2.1
2	Packing/marketing	4.20.1.2	4.20.2.2
3	Storage costs	4.20.1.3	4.20.2.3
4	Post harvest losses	4.20.1.4	4.20.2.4
5	Other (pls. specify ....)	4.20.1.5	4.20.2.5

District Code: _____ ; Household ID: _____

Section 5: Access and extension services – All questions concern the last 12 months

	A For crop production	B For livestock activities
5.1.0 Do you get information and advice from extension workers? **KEY for 5.1.0:** 1 yes; 2 no	5.1.0a	5.1.0b
5.1.1 How many times do they visit you per year?	5.1.1a	5.1.1b
5.1.2 Do you pay for receiving extension advice? **KEY for 5.1.2:** 1 yes; 2 no *(If no, go to Question 5.1.4)*	5.1.2a	5.1.2b
5.1.3 How much do you pay annually for extension?	5.1.3a	5.1.3b
5.1.4 The extension officials who visit/contact you are from which organization?	5.1.4a	5.1.4b
KEY for 5.1.4:　1 Government agency; 　　　　　　　2 Agriculture research station; 　　　　　　　3 NGO; 　　　　　　　4 Other (pls. specify ...).		

5.2.1 Have extension officers provided information on expected rainfall and precipitation? _____
KEY for 5.2: 1 yes; 2 no
5.3 If you get any technical assistance and advice from other sources apart from official extension workers, from where do you receive the necessary information? _____
KEY for 5.3: 1 Media; 2 Neighbouring farmer; 3 Shopkeepers in village; 4 Others (pls. specify ...); 5 None.

District Code: _____ ; Household ID: _____

Section 6: Household finance

6.1 What is the **total** household net income from farm activities (own or someone else's farm) in the **last 12 months**? _____ (NB: use income table if necessary)

6.1.1 Over the **last 12 months**, what **percentage** of total household net income is from **non-farm** activities (e.g. income (salary) from non-agriculture activities and other sources such as gifts, pensions, etc.)?: _____

6.2 What is the **total** net household income from farm activities *in* a **normal average year**? _____ (NB: use income table if necessary)

6.2.1 In a **normal average year**, what **percentage** of total household net income is from **non-farm** activities (e.g. income (salary) from non-agriculture activities and other sources such as gifts, pensions, etc.)?: _____

6.3 How much has your household paid for the following over the last 12 months?

6.3.1	Income taxes	
6.3.2	Property taxes	
6.3.3	Sales taxes	
6.3.4	Other costs (pls. specify …)	

6.4 Did you borrow from any of the following sources for farming over the last 12 months?

6.4.0 Source	6.4.1 Borrowed from: (1 yes; 2 no)	6.4.2 Amount received	6.4.3 Interest rate/year	6.4.4 Repayment over how many months/years
1 Relatives/friends	6.4.1.1	6.4.2.1	6.4.3.1	6.4.4.1
2 Farmer associations/cooperatives	6.4.1.2	6.4.2.2	6.4.3.2	6.4.4.2
3 Commercial banks	6.4.1.3	6.4.2.3	6.4.3.3	6.4.4.3
4 Thrift and loan society	6.4.1.4	6.4.2.4	6.4.3.4	6.4.4.4
5 Others (Pls. specify)	6.4.1.5	6.4.2.5	6.4.3.5	6.4.4.5

6.5 Have you received any of the following types of subsidies during the last 12 months?

	6.5.1 (1 yes; 2 no)	6.5.2 Source	6.5.3 Amount/year
1 Crop subsidy	6.5.1.1	6.5.2.1	6.5.3.1
2 Input subsidy	6.5.1.2	6.5.2.2	6.5.3.2
3 Direct payment	6.5.1.3	6.5.2.3	6.5.3.3
4 Other (Pls. specify type _____)	6.5.1.4	6.5.2.4	6.5.3.4

KEY for 6.5.2: 1 From the government;
2 From NGO;
3 From private sector sources;
4 From other (Pls. specify source).

District Code: _____; Household ID: _____

Section 7: Adaptation options

7.0 How long have you been a farmer (or farm manager)? _____ (in number of years)

Short-term climate effects

7.1 What are the households' **adaptation strategies to climatic variation** (e.g. **weather effects** in terms of temperature and rainfall fluctuations, wind, dust storms, etc.) within and betweens seasons?

7.2 What are the main primary constraints for making the necessary adjustments **to climatic variation** (e.g. **weather effects** in terms of temperature and rainfall fluctuations, wind, dust storms, etc.) within and betweens seasons?

Long-term climate change

7.3 Have you noticed any long-term shifts in the mean temperature on your farm? (please explain)

7.4 Have you noticed any long-term shifts in the mean rainfall on your farm? (please explain)

7.5 What adjustments in your farming have you made to these long-term shifts in temperature? Please list below.

7.6 What adjustments in your farming have you made to these long-term shifts in rainfall? Please list below.

District Code: _____ ; Household ID: _____

This section **must** be completed after the interview is completed. Given the importance of the following data for mapping and tracking purposes, please ensure it is filled out accurately.

Instructions: This section to be filled out by interviewer
Name of interviewer:
_____

Time interview ended:
(this information is important to validate survey responses and will be used to cross check in the event that there are unusual observations during the analysis of the data)

Date of interview (mm/dd/yr)

Respondent households' identification number
(unique household ID should be assigned
prior to interview)
(1 interview 1; 2 interview 2; ... n survey
n for each district)

Location of farm

Country

Province/region

District

District code
(as provided by Yale)

Subdivision/division

Village

Optional: Contact information of respondent: _____

_____

(address)

District Code: _____; Household ID: _____

Index

*For Product Safety Concerns and Information please contact
our EU representative GPSR@taylorandfrancis.com Taylor & Francis
Verlag GmbH, Kaufingerstraße 24, 80331 München, Germany*

T - #0086 - 230425 - C16 - 234/156/11 - PB - 9780415852838 - Gloss Lamination